The Habsburg
Legacy
1867–1939

Franz Joseph (1830–1916), Emperor-King of Austria-Hungary. Painting by Wasmuth. *(Verlag-Wolfsberger, Vienna)*

The Habsburg
Legacy
1867–1939

BRUCE F. PAULEY
Florida Technological University

Holt, Rinehart and Winston, Inc.
New York   Chicago   San Francisco   Atlanta
Dallas   Montreal   Toronto   London   Sydney

To my father
who encouraged me to take up
the study of history

Preface

East Central Europe has witnessed some of the most dramatic events of the twentieth century: the First World War, the collapse of a great empire, the formation of new nation-states, the confrontation of nationalities, the rise of National Socialism, diplomatic crises in the late 1930s, and the outbreak of World War II. Yet many Americans still know as little about the lands between Germany and Russia as did the British Prime Minister Neville Chamberlain, who just before the Munich Conference bemoaned the possibility of a war occurring over a "quarrel in a faraway country between people of whom we know nothing."

Much of what has been written on East Central Europe has done little to lift the fog of ignorance, as it is misleading at best, partisan and polemical at worst. The Habsburg Monarchy, for example, has received a poor "press" in the Western democracies, at least until recent years. Multinational, authoritarian, Roman Catholic, predominantly agricultural, more devoted to the fine arts than to profit, it once appeared to all progressive and nationalistic observers to be defiantly reactionary, the "prison of the peoples." The "Successor States" which replaced it, on the other hand, baptized in nationalism and democracy, were greeted as welcome additions to the modern world. Their conquest by the Nazis and Soviets assured them of continuing sympathy in a West haunted by feelings of guilt at having abandoned them in 1938–1939.

Most works on East Central Europe have either ended or begun with the year 1918, thus leaving the reader wondering what happened to the fragments of the Austro-Hungarian Monarchy, or confused by the bewildering domestic and foreign problems confronting the Successor States. This book is dedicated to the proposition that neither the Monarchy nor its legacy can be properly understood without careful comparisons between the pre–World War I and interwar years.

A number of friends and colleagues have graciously contributed valuable ideas and suggestions to this study. My thanks go to Robert J. Parks, Thomas C. Kennedy, and William Epstein of the University of Wyoming, and Eric C. Kollman of Cornell College. I am especially grateful to the editor of this series, Professor Keith Eubank of Queens College, whose constructive observations have eased the preparation of this book. For whatever mistakes in fact or judgment may be found in these pages, I am, of course, entirely responsible.

Orlando, Fla.   B. F. P.
November 1971

Contents

Maps

CHAPTER ONE

The Multinational Empire

The Evolution of the Habsburg Monarchy, 1526–1867

The dual state of Austria Hungary was a late nineteenth-century museum piece. After 1871 it was one of the only three major European states (along with Russia and the Ottoman Empire) not organized on a national basis. The Habsburg Monarchy, or simply Austria, as it was frequently but inaccurately called, bore a striking resemblance to a medieval feudal state. A loose confederation of territories varying in size, national composition, and history, the principal tie of its components was a common allegiance to a single monarch. To a rigorously logical mind, the Dual Monarchy was an absurd anachronism.

The Monarchy's peculiar structure was the

product of a historical evolution dating back to the sixteenth century. Habsburg rule over South German lands began in 1278, but the birth date of the Monarchy as a multinational state is 1526. In that year the diets (parliaments) of Bohemia and Hungary, threatened by Turkish invasion, elected Ferdinand I (1519–1564), Archduke of Austria since 1519, as their king. But during the sixteenth and seventeenth centuries the Habsburgs were too distracted by the Turks, French, and Protestants, as well as by the Thirty Years' War, to consolidate their new possessions. So, at a time when England and France were becoming centralized nation-states, the Habsburg Monarchy remained politically backward.

The prenationalistic eighteenth century was probably the last period in which Austria might have been converted into a homogeneous nation-state. Instead, by the 1770s it was more diversified than ever. When the century began, Magyars in the Hungarian plain had just been reconquered from the Ottoman Turks. In 1742 most of the large and densely populated German-speaking province of Silesia was lost to Prussia. Thirty years later, a huge slice of southern Poland called Galicia was acquired by Austria in the first partition of Poland.

The attempts of Maria Theresa (1740–1780) and her son Joseph II (1780–1790) to impose uniformity on their lands were only partially successful. As an enlightened despot Joseph was eager to create an efficient and centralized administration; but his objective necessitated an official language. That language could only be German, since it was the one vernacular tongue with more than local usage. But Joseph's brief reign demonstrated that centralization could not be distinguished from Germanization. And centralization would inevitably be resisted in the name of "state's rights" *(Staatsrecht),* or "historic rights." Anything resembling Germanization would stimulate national consciousness among non-German Austrians. Joseph's reforms ended with rebellions in the Austrian Netherlands and Hungary. Austria's most cosmopolitan ruler thus ironically played a major role in the rise of modern nationalism in the Habsburg Monarchy.

Until Joseph's reign, the nationality question had been

practically nonexistent. Only those nationalities with a separate history (usually called the historic nations) dating from the Middle Ages had any self-consciousness, and even then it was confined to the aristocracy in the case of the Poles, Magyars, and Croatians, and to the aristocracy and a small middle class in the case of the Germans and Italians. The "nonhistoric nationalities" (Slovenes and Ruthenes in Austria, and Slovaks, Rumanians, and Serbs in Hungary) consisted almost exclusively of peasants who were largely indifferent to nationalism before 1848. The Czechs fell between the two categories, having a separate and even glorious medieval history, but lacking a nationally conscious aristocracy or national independence since the early seventeenth century. For nearly two hundred years they remained a peasant people, hardly distinguishable from the nonhistoric nations.

Habsburg nationalities, awakened by Joseph's centralizing policies, were further aroused by the French Revolution. The Empire survived countless defeats and territorial mutilations but could not remain immune from the revolutionary principles of government by consent and the abolition of feudal privileges and divine rights. Even the desperate attempt to resist the revolutionary ideology by Austria's foreign minister, Prince Clemens von Metternich (1809–1848), ended in failure.

Metternich's restrictions on civil liberties embittered the small liberal minority of industrialists, factory workers, students, and professional people and helped spark the Revolutions of 1848. The course of the revolutions, however, revealed that nationalism rather than liberalism was the deepest source of discontent in the Monarchy. Nationalistic disturbances broke out in the Hungarian capital of Pressburg (Bratislava), Vienna, Prague, Milan, and Venice, but were all crushed by the autumn of 1849. The same fate awaited the popularly elected constituent assembly meeting in Kremsier (Moravia) which in a rare display of national compromise drew up a constitution that combined the historic rights of crownlands with new demands for ethnic autonomy. National *Kreise* (circles) were to be created within the crownlands to protect minorities. But the new eighteen-year-old emperor, Franz Joseph I (1848–1916), and his prime minis-

Franz Joseph in 1848. Painting by Anton Einsle. *(Heeresgeschicht-liches Museum, Vienna)*

ter, Felix Schwarzenberg, would have nothing to do with the constitution's theory of popular sovereignty and restored the absolutistic old regime. In so doing they may have destroyed the last or at least best opportunity to settle the nationality issue peacefully.

In the years following the revolutions Austria reverted to the centralism of the Josephinian period. Provincial automony was virtually eliminated, even for Hungary. State officials now had to be fluent in German, and German was increasingly made the language of education. The ideal of Minister of the Interior Alexander Bach was essentially the same as Joseph's: efficient administration and equal treatment for all nationalities. The German Austrians were given no special consideration; nevertheless centralization had all the appearances of Germanization to the non-German nationalities. The German-speaking Austrians also came to think of the state as essentially German. If they were given no more political or civil privileges than other nationalities, they at least enjoyed the satisfaction of knowing theirs was the language of state, education, and culture. This situation they accepted as the norm; the later rise in use of non-German languages was regarded as a threat to the state and their position in it.

Centralism in the 1850s had even slimmer prospects of success than in the far less nationalistic 1780s. Once more, the attempt to turn Austria into a modern state led to resistance and soon had to be abandoned.

The Compromise of 1867

Since the Magyars were the most important opponents of any centralized government, Franz Joseph attempted to reach an understanding with their spokesman, Ferencz Deák. Negotiations began in 1865 but were stalled by Austria's defeat at the hands of Prussia the following year. Now the Emperor's preoccupation was internal consolidation in order to gain quick revenge on Germany. Consequently, he conceded more to the Magyars than he might have under more favorable circumstances.

The resulting Compromise, or *Ausgleich,* of 1867 assured Hungary of complete independence in internal affairs such as justice, education, and transportation, as well as an equal voice in common imperial affairs involving defense, diplomacy, and joint finance. In exchange, Hungary was required to pay only a third of the joint expenses. The Magyars gained control over Hungary proper, Croatia, the largely Serb area of Voivodina, and the predominantly Rumanian province of Transylvania. In all, well over half the territory of the Dual Monarchy was placed under Magyar hegemony, even though the Magyars made up little more than one-fifth of the Monarchy's population. As it turned out, however, Franz Joseph was "killing" the Magyars with kindness in giving them more minorities than they could possibly absorb.

Under the terms of the *Ausgleich* the two countries had a common ruler, Franz Joseph, who was King of Hungary and Emperor of "Austria" (the name usually, though not officially given to the non-Hungarian parts of the Monarchy). He was the Commander-in-Chief of the common army; he appointed the common ministers of war, foreign affairs, and finance, and the separate state ministers of Austria and Hungary. The two states had a single tariff adjusted every ten years by mutual agreement by representatives of the Austrian and Hungarian parliaments. Here again, Hungary was allowed an equal share of power. A joint parliament was never created, moreover, because the Magyars feared that Hungary might play a subordinate role.

Finally, any constitutional changes in Austria or Hungary could be blocked by either state. In practice this stipulation meant that the Magyars could prevent any attempt to federalize either Austria or the whole Dual Monarchy, as was seen in Franz Joseph's unsuccessful effort to grant Bohemia autonomy in 1871. Having now achieved the limits of their aspirations within the Monarchy, the Magyars were determined to prevent the realization of other national ambitions lest their own position be weakened. It was this aspect of the Compromise which was later to place it in ill repute.

When it was concluded, the *Ausgleich* reflected the im-

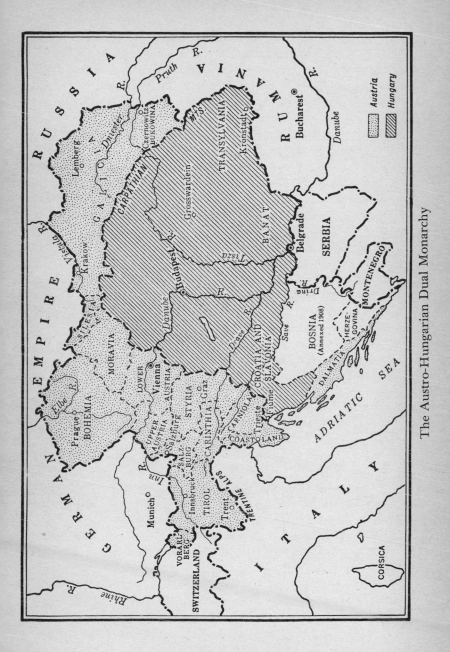

The Austro-Hungarian Dual Monarchy

portance of the Monarchy's two leading nationalities. The German Austrians and Magyars were the only two peoples with the administrative experience for self-government; in addition, they owned the greater part of the land and industry in the Habsburg state. Within a few decades, however, these same nationalities had lost some of their relative advantages to the smaller nationalities, and the *Ausgleich* came to look more and more obsolete to objective observers.

Despite the predominant political status assured them by the Compromise, the Germans and Magyars were minorities in both Austria and Hungary. To strengthen their political grip, both made "deals" with the second-ranking nationalities of their respective states. The Poles of Austrian Galicia were given administrative (but not legislative) autonomy; state officials in the crownland were to be Poles and the Polish language was to be used instead of German in the Galician schools and universities. In exchange, the Poles tacitly agreed to support the German Austrians in the Vienna government. This arrangement worked smoothly until 1918. The Magyars, for their part, agreed to give Croatia limited legislative and wide administrative autonomy but hedged both concessions by insisting that the Croatian governor was to be appointed by the Hungarian government in its new capital of Budapest. This so-called *Nagodba,* or Compromise of 1868, satisfied neither side completely and began to break down in the twentieth century.

The Democratization of Austria, 1879–1907

The dominant theme in Austrian (but not Hungarian) politics after 1867 was the gradual extension of political, cultural, and economic equality to all nationalities, particularly during the ministry of Count Eduard von Taaffe (1879–1893). Heading a coalition composed of clericals, German aristocrats, and conservative Czechs, the Premier persuaded all nationalities, including the recalcitrant Czechs, to attend the Reichsrat (the Imperial Parliament of Austria). In 1882 he pushed through a franchise reform which increased the number of urban voters by 34 percent and rural voters by 26 percent. He divided the

University of Prague into Czech and German sections and induced Parliament to pass a law requiring the political, administrative, and judicial authorities of Bohemia to use the language
of the parties concerned. The Czechs profited enormously from
this law as well as from a franchise reform in Bohemia giving
them control of the provincial diet. Beneficial to the lower
middle-class and industrial workers in all parts of Austria was
social insurance, which also encouraged the moderate "revisionist" wing of the Austrian labor movement.

Taaffe has often been criticized for not finding a "solution"

NATIONALITIES IN AUSTRIA-HUNGARY

Germans	Slovenes	Slovaks
Czechs	Serbo-Croats	Italians

Ruthenians	Magyars
Rumanians	Poles

0   40   80   120
Miles

to the nationality problem. Paradoxically, his failure even to seek one was the secret of his successful fourteen-year administration, by far the longest in the history of Imperial Austria. Knowing that if any one nationality were completely satisfied, another one would be infuriated, he strove to keep all nationalities in a state of "well-balanced discontent." His interest in pragmatic deeds rather than ideology, together with his sense of humor, kept the national struggle subdued during his many years in office.

Two years after Taaffe fell from power his coalition was revived under the premiership of Count Kasimir Badeni, a Polish aristocrat. Unlike Taaffe, Badeni had little knowledge of Austria outside his native Galicia and, worse, he was reluctant to seek advice. His parochialism, along with his dependence on Czech support, led him to publish two notorious language ordinances in April 1897. They decreed that after July 1901 all civil servants in Bohemia and Moravia would be required to know both Czech and German. In theory the regulations provided for absolute equality of the two nationalities: Czech officials in purely Czech areas would be required to know German, and German officials in purely German areas would have to speak Czech. In practice, however, the decrees favored the Czechs, since nearly all educated members of that nationality already knew German. By the same token, few Germans had any command of Czech. If put into effect the regulations would have led to large numbers of German-speaking officials being replaced by Czechs. But they had even wider implications: once the principle of complete bilingualism was established in the Czech provinces, other small nationalities would expect the same treatment for themselves and the leading position of the German Austrians would be undermined.

Even if Badeni had maneuvered with infinite tact, the new rulings would have been offensive to most German-speaking Austrians. As it was, he aggravated the situation by ignoring parliamentary sanctions and issuing the language ordinances as decrees. When the German deputies in the Reichsrat could not muster the votes to overthrow the Premier, they turned to boisterous filibustering and violence on the chamber floor. Pan-

German extremists in German-Bohemia, Vienna, and Graz took to the streets.

The Badeni crisis marked the beginning of the last and most volatile phase of the nationality conflict in Austria. The uproar was a devastating blow to parliamentarianism and the prestige of the Monarchy itself. German Austrian chauvinism quickly spread to other nationalities through the new mass circulation press. Foreigners, seeing only the most disruptive aspects of Austrian political life, began to speculate about the "inevitability" of Austria's disintegration.

Franz Joseph attempted to revive parliamentary life and simultaneously to lessen national conflicts in 1907 when he encouraged the Reichsrat to broaden the franchise to include all male citizens over twenty-four. Count Taaffe had already persuaded the Emperor of the need for such reform, and the Russian revolution of 1905 made the change seem all the more imperative. This was no proof that the Emperor had become a devoted advocate of democracy at the age of seventy-seven; as usual, he was looking for ways to consolidate the state and thereby improve its power position in Europe. In a sense he was also returning to the mentality of Joseph II in believing that the lower classes were basically more loyal to the dynasty than was the urban middle class. The former were presumably more concerned about social and economic problems than national and constitutional questions. This idea was not unreasonable, since many national movements originated within and continued to draw their strongest support from the middle class. As late as 1848 peasants were interested in emancipation and little else. The same could not be said, however, of the urban masses in the early twentieth century, or for that matter even of some peasants.

In addition to universal manhood suffrage, the franchise reform provided for 516 Reichsrat seats to be distributed among the nationalities roughly according to population, with adjustments for cultural and economic considerations. The German Austrians, although still having the largest representation, voluntarily gave up their absolute majority.

The elections of 1907 seemed to vindicate the most optimistic hopes of the proponents of suffrage reform. The Christian Social and the Social Democratic parties were the two largest emerging from the balloting. Both were supporters of the Monarchy and in theory, at least, antinationalistic. Between them they garnered 184 representatives, or more than one-third of the total. A majority government was formed which obtained passage of the budget and the decennial adjustment of the common tariff with Hungary.

The apparent triumph of democracy was short lived. Of the Reichsrat's twenty-eight factions and seventeen major parties, all but the Christian Social and the Social Democratic parties were based on nationality. Collectively they were even less responsible than the unreformed Parliament. The new Lower House, in fact, degenerated into little more than a circus. For once, Adolf Hitler was not far wrong in his youthful impression of the assembly:

> The intellectual content of what these men said was on a really depressing level, in so far as you could understand their babbling at all; for several of the gentlemen did not speak German. . . . A wild gesticulating mass screaming all at once in every different key, presided over by a good natured old uncle who was striving in the sweat of his brow to revive the dignity of the House by violently ringing his bell and alternating gentle reproof with grave admonitions.[1]

Such a spectacle did little to enhance Hitler's respect for parliamentary democracy. Other observers, although less sarcastic, basically shared the future Nazi leader's assessment. The American journalist Wolf von Schierbrand wrote:

> . . . For there is a total absence of dignity and efficiency there, and the bulk of the 500 delegates or thereabouts whom I saw on entering the press gallery looked and behaved like a band of madmen. . . . About a score of men, all decently clad, were seated or standing each at his little desk. Some made an infernal noise violently opening and shutting the lids of their desks. Others emitted a blaring sound from little toy trumpets; others strummed on Jew's harps; still others beat snare drums. . . . Every other [faction] . . . had stored away . . . a complete assort-

[1] *Mein Kampf* (Boston: Houghton Mifflin, 1943), p. 77.

ment of such instruments of torture—whistles and sleigh bells,
mouth harmonicas, cow bells and trombones, specially manufactured noise-producers warranted to overtop everything . . . .
merely for the purpose of making all legitimate business in the
Reichsrat impossible. . . .²

A complete list of abusive expressions used in the Lower Chamber was published in 1902 and consisted of no fewer than 1763
terms ranging from "ass" to "zebra."

Fortunately the governing of Austria was not dependent
on such theatrics. The state machine continued to run smoothly,
well oiled by the civil bureaucracy. The absolutistic powers
surrendered by Franz Joseph half a century earlier were partially restored, meaning that more democracy in theory meant
less in practice. Productive political work took place after 1907
but not in Vienna; rather it was in the provincial diets where
the franchise reform had not been introduced. If the franchise
reform proved anything, it was the ungovernability of Austria
along democratic lines, at least while the political parties sub-
ordinated imperial questions to national self-interest.

Nationality Problems in Austria

Nationalism, which emasculated the Austrian Reichsrat
and which ultimately helped to destroy the Austro-Hungarian
Monarchy, sharply increased in intensity during the second half
of the nineteenth century. A major reason was economic. The
emancipation of the serfs in 1848 led to dramatic changes in
economic relations between historic and nonhistoric nationalities. With their new freedom of movement peasants began mi-
grating to the larger towns and cities that were beginning to
industrialize. Previously German-speaking communities became
largely Slav or Magyar within a generation or two, Prague and
Budapest being the most outstanding examples. Although this
transformation was nearly completed by 1880, the process made
an indelible imprint on the mentality of many Habsburg Germans (including the young Hitler), who resented and resisted

² *Austria-Hungary, The Polyglot Empire* (New York: Frederick A. Stokes, 1917),
pp. 116–117.

the de-Germanization of the Empire. Conservatism thus became an almost instinctive ideology with many German Austrians.

As the economic and cultural standards of less developed nationalities rose, so too did their sense of nationalism. The more nationalistic they became, the more oppressed they felt. So the most dangerous national movement, for example, belonged to the Magyars, even though they were almost completely independent in domestic affairs. The Czechs were equally restless, despite winning concession after concession from the Austrian government and enjoying a standard of living only slightly inferior to that of the German Austrians. By contrast, the Ruthenes and Slovaks had miserable living standards and in Hungary practically no political rights, yet they had no national self-consciousness or sense of oppression worth mentioning.

Nationalist and even Socialist critics of the Habsburg Empire both before and after the First World War often charged that national unrest was due to Germanization, discriminatory laws and governmental policies, or "divide and rule" techniques. All three accusations missed the mark insofar as the Austrian half of the Dual Monarchy was concerned. The question of Germanization has already been discussed in connection with Joseph II and Alexander Bach, both of whom were simply interested in efficient administration. The Habsburgs themselves never had a policy of Germanization. They pragmatically favored whichever nationality was most loyal at any given moment. What Germanization did take place was confined almost exclusively to the pre-1848 era and resulted from the cultural and economic appeal of the German nationality rather than government policies. There were, of course, Pan-Germans who would have been delighted with forced Germanization, but they were neither numerous nor successful in their programs. They are remembered mainly as forerunners of the National Socialists and as a group that provided Austrophobes with useful propaganda.

Where the Germanization charge contains an element of truth is in the prestige that the German language and culture retained in Austria and to some extent in Hungary, to the end of the Monarchy. Only one-fourth of the inhabitants of the dual state spoke German as their native tongue, but millions more mastered it as a second language. Even Slavic nationalists, as a practical necessity, were forced to use it. Well over half the newspapers and periodicals of Austria were printed in German; nearly half the university students spoke German, as did 80 percent of the members of the central ministries of the Austrian government and 75 percent of the officers in the Austro-Hungarian army. The German Austrians also continued to look upon themselves as the *Staatsvolk* (people of state) rather than just another nationality. Superficially, then, the Austrian half of the Monarchy had a German appearance as late as 1918.

German predominance was due to a fortunate historical development rather than to discrimination. The German Austrians were the only large Austrian nationality speaking a language of European stature. They had always been closer to the cultural, economic, and intellectual centers of Western Europe than any of the other Austrian nationalities, except the Czechs, and had been one of the few nationalities of East Central Europe to escape Turkish domination. They also profited from their plurality and geographic dispersion throughout most parts of the Monarchy.

The accusation concerning legal or political discrimination is also distorted at best. After 1907 the non-German nationalities were not only represented in the Reichsrat on a roughly proportional basis, but they also enjoyed complete equality in educational and cultural institutions. Any possible discrimination resulted from occasional administrative inefficiencies rather than prejudicial laws.

It is true that "divide and rule" techniques were employed by the Habsburgs from time to time to take advantage of national jealousies. The emperor Franz I (1792–1835), for example, was quoted as saying: "My people are strangers to each other, and so much the better. I send Hungarians to Italy and Italians to Hungary. From their antipathy arises order and from their many-sided hatred, peace."[3] But these enmities by no means depended on the Habsburgs. They not only lingered on after

---

[3] Ernst Fischer, *Österreich 1848; Probleme der demokratischen Revolution in Österreich* (Vienna: Stern Verlag, 1946), p. 130.

the departure of the dynasty, but intensified. There is no reason to doubt that the Habsburgs would have been more than happy to please all nationalities at once; the tragedy was that this was impossible. Concessions to one group were immediately interpreted as insults by another. So the Habsburgs satisfied the largest and most important nationalities, who in most cases were the historic nationalities. In a sense the policy was democratic, since the majority "ruled." Understandably this fact was cold comfort to the less privileged nations.

Despite their acid denunciations of Habsburg policies few of the nationalities of either half of the Monarchy wished to secede before the outbreak of the First World War. Dread of the unknown and doubt as to whether anything better could take the place of the Monarchy were firmly imprinted in the psyche of the average Austrian. Moreover, none of the Czechs and only insignificant numbers of German Austrians had any desire to be swallowed up in a Greater Germany. The Poles preferred Austrian to German or Russian rule at a time when complete Polish independence seemed a fantasy. Ruthenes, Rumanians, and Magyars were all terrified of Russia, and the Slovenes preferred Austria to neighboring Italy. Only some Serbs and Italians looked longingly at their nationals in neighboring nation-states. And neither of these nationalities was essential to the existence of Austria-Hungary, since each was small and peripheral.

No Austrian nationality was completely satisfied with its status, but only the Czechs presented a serious threat to the state. And of the Czechs, only those of Bohemia, were highly dissatisfied. Paradoxically, by the early twentieth century the Czechs were the most advanced Slavs in the world culturally and economically. They had the highest literacy rate (over 97 percent) in either Austria or Hungary, and Bohemia was economically by far the most important crownland in the Austrian half of the Monarchy. Even before 1900 it supplied a quarter of Austria's revenue. Moreover, unlike Galicia or the Italian possessions, Bohemia was no outlying province, but part of the vital heartland of the Dual Monarchy. Without it Austria-Hungary could hardly hope to be a great power.

The essence of the Bohemian enigma lay in its bilingual character. No less than a third of its inhabitants, most of them living along the perimeter, were German-speaking. Any major concession to the Czechs invariably offended this largest and most important Austrian nationality.

The first serious demand for home rule was made at the Kremsier Parliament in 1848 when the Czech leader and historian Františeck Palacký modestly asked for autonomy for Czech-speaking areas, thus renouncing the idea of "historic unity" in the Bohemian crownlands (Bohemia, Moravia, and Austrian Silesia). He did, however, broach the idea of a Czech-Slovak union within the Monarchy. By 1867 the Czechs had grown far more self-confident and escalated their program to autonomy for the whole of the Bohemian crownlands. Thereafter they regarded all three provinces as legitimate areas for "reconquest"; they considered the Germans as "colonists" (even though they had been living in the region since the thirteenth century) and fit material for conversion to the Czech nationality, or at best toleration as a minority.

The German Bohemians, on the other hand, considered themselves a *Herrenvolk* (master race) and naturally superior to the Czechs, whose language was a "mere dialect suitable only for peasants and servants." The Germans insisted that Austria remain a centralized state in which they would outnumber the Czechs. Neither nationality recognized the legitimacy of the other's political ambitions and both saw their rivals as actual or at least potential traitors. The Czechs were fond of blocking constructive legislation in Vienna, and the German Bohemians took delight in obstructing the provincial diet in Prague. The Czechs were strong enough in the Bohemian capital to prevent administrative autonomy from being given to the Germans, and the Germans had enough power in Vienna to preclude the realization of the Czechs' *Staatsrecht* program of autonomy for the whole of the Bohemian crownlands.

An element of reason was introduced into the dispute in the early years of the twentieth century when Thomas G. Masaryk, a philosophy professor at the Czech University of Prague, founded a new party known as the Realists. Although it never achieved numerical importance, Masaryk soon gained prominence as a high-minded idealist. He returned to Palacký's 1848 program of ethnic autonomy and union with the Slovaks and ignored "historic rights." Time after time Masaryk rose in the Reichsrat to denounce the idea of complete Czech independence and to reaffirm his belief in Austria's future, a conviction shared by his student and future collaborator, Edvard Beneš.

Some of Masaryk's speeches now make strange reading in view of his later role as the father of an independent Czechoslovak state. In his official party program of 1900, for example, he announced:

> We believe that the previous complete independence of the Bohemian lands is impossible. Our limited number of inhabitants, our inland position, and the fact that the Bohemian lands are inhabited also by German and Polish populations forced us in the past and force us still into an association with other nationalities and other states.[4]

In one of his last Reichsrat speeches in 1913 Masaryk still insisted: "No one can deny who knows the clear and obvious facts, that our nation has in Austria the relatively best conditions for its cultural, political and economic development."[5]

No solution to the Bohemian problem was ever found before the war, although negotiations for a settlement continued until the start of hostilities. But the two sides were sometimes very close to agreement and might have eventually reached it through sheer exhaustion alone.

Nationality Problems in Hungary

The nearest analogy to the Bohemian embroilment was found in Hungary. The Magyars, like the Czechs, constituted only a precarious majority in their kingdom, and then only if

[4] Quoted in Dagmar H. Perman, *The Shaping of the Czechoslovak State: Diplomatic Boundaries of Czechoslovakia* (Leiden: E. J. Brill, 1962), pp. 12–13.
[5] Quoted in Hugo Hantsch, *Die Geschichte Österreichs,* vol. II, *1648–1918* (Graz: Verlag Styria, 1953), p. 531.

the Croats were excluded from the tally. Both Magyars and Czechs benefited from occupying central lowlands, whereas their minorities lived on poorer, mountainous soil along the fringes of the state. The Magyars, like the Czechs, had a strong sense of historical continuity and used it to justify their lordship over minority peoples. Both had struggled against the Habsburgs since 1526. But here the similarities ended. The bearer of Magyar nationalism was the aristocracy, giving it a strong conservative tinge in social matters. Czech nationalism was cultivated by the middle class and therefore tended to be liberal and democratic. The Magyars were more fortunate than the Czechs in being faced with not one powerful minority, but several small and weak ones. The most important difference between the two nationalities, of course, was the Magyars' ability to maintain their autonomy throughout the centuries.

The history of the Hungarian state between 1867 and 1914 is essentially the history of the Magyars' attempt to assimilate, or at least suppress their many minorities. Unlike Germans and Slavs in the Dual Monarchy, the Magyars had no ethnic allies. Pan-Germanism and Pan-Slavism had no counterpart for the Magyars, causing them to feel isolated and threatened. They believed, not without some justification, that either they would rule over and assimilate their minorities, or they would in turn be subjugated by them.

This phobia was not limited to a handful of chauvinists. The Magyars almost without exception upheld the absolute indivisibility of the state and the need to absorb minorities. Differences arose only over techniques. During the first few years following the conclusion of the *Ausgleich* a generous nationality law was enforced to facilitate gradual and voluntary assimilation. But after 1876 it became a dead letter, being replaced by an accelerated policy of forced Magyarization stifling nearly all expressions of national life among the minorities. Franchise laws were so discriminatory that the lesser nationalities (excluding the Croats) never obtained more than 27 out of 413 seats in the Hungarian Diet. Public schools, especially beyond the primary level, were almost nonexistent except for

German Hungarians, although private minority schools were left alone. The Magyars supplied over 90 percent of all government employees, secondary teachers, and university instructors, most of whom treated the minorities with contempt. Railroads and highways were built to lead toward Budapest and hinder travel to foreign countries, even to Austria.

Such policies achieved considerable success by 1914. Whereas Magyar was spoken by only 40-42 percent of the Hungarian population in the 1840s and 1850s, the figure had risen to nearly 55 percent by 1910. In the urban centers the change was even more dramatic, with over three-quarters of the population speaking Magyar.

The impact of Magyarization varied substantially among the various nationalities. The Germans and Jews accepted it most readily, followed by the Slovaks and Ruthenes. Even enemies of the Magyars admitted that these nationalities probably would have been fully assimilated within another twenty to fifty years if the First World War and the partitioning of Hungary had not intervened. Rumanians, Serbs, and Croats, on the other hand, resisted Magyarization and succeeded in increasing their absolute numbers, although their percentage of the total population declined somewhat.

However harsh Magyarization *methods* may have been, several points can be made in defense of the policy itself. The Magyars were not unique in seeking to assimilate their minorities. The same ambition existed at this time in Russia and Germany. In an age of extreme nationalism, full national unity was considered as essential as religious uniformity had been during the Reformation. Discrimination against minorities, moreover, was purely political in Hungary; the minorities benefited from the industrialization which took place after 1880. The Slovaks, in particular, were favored through government investments. Likewise, racial discrimination was not practiced. Once a German, a Jew, or a Slovak accepted Magyar culture his ethnic background was ignored and he became a bona fide member of Magyar society. It would also be a mistake to assume that discriminatory policies, deeply offensive to a Czech or an Italian in Austria, were necessarily resented by Hungarian minorities.

Many of these actually welcomed the opportunity to Magyarize themselves as a means of escaping their rustic backgrounds and entering a more sophisticated way of life. On the negative side, however, it is likely that extreme Magyar chauvinism reduced rather than increased the number of potential converts. And it discredited Hungary, and even the whole Dual Monarchy, abroad.

Of the nationality movements in pre–World War I Hungary, only the Croatian, Serbian, and Rumanian can be considered in any way to have been a menace to the state. In the case of the Croatians, however, their relations with the Magyars were better in 1914 than in 1907; and though the "Yugoslav" idea was growing (that is, the union of all Habsburg South Slavs and the Serbs of Serbia in a common state), its adherents among the Croats were a minority. To most Roman Catholic Croats, not to mention Slovenes, the idea of joining the economically and culturally backward Eastern Orthodox Serbs was unappealing if not repulsive. These considerations, of course, did not exist for Habsburg Serbs, who differed from their nationals in the Kingdom of Serbia only in being more prosperous and better educated. The secessionist impulse among Serbs in the Monarchy was therefore undoubtedly strong.

A similarity in culture could also be found among the Rumanians of Austria-Hungary and those in the Kingdom of Rumania (the Regat). The more articulate Rumanians of Hungary (but not Austria) favored leaving the Monarchy in 1914, although they were probably a minority at this time. But their number had been growing since the failure to introduce universal manhood suffrage in Hungary in 1905.

It would be no exaggeration to say that the integrity of the Austro-Hungarian Empire in 1914 was threatened less by the nationality movements in Hungary, or even the much stronger ones in Austria, than by Magyar nationalism itself. The *Ausgleich* had left the Magyars in control of not only their own destiny but also that of huge minorities. At the same time they enjoyed the protection of the joint army against foreign enemies. Even so, the more extreme of the Magyar nationalists were not content. The aging rebel of 1848, Lajos Kossuth, pitted his enormous prestige against any association with the Habsburgs until his dying day in 1894. After the turn of the century the Independence party grew in strength at the very time when Hungary was prospering from its economic connection with Austria. It was characteristic of dyed-in-the-wool nationalists everywhere, however, not to be troubled by mundane matters like economic survival.

The Imperial Dynasty

Austria-Hungary's nationality problem has attracted so much attention that it is tempting to ignore the many elements holding the Dual Monarchy together. Of these, the Habsburg dynasty deserves a category of its own.

Monarchism was a principle easily understood by even the most simple-minded peasant. It avoided the abstract nature of nationalism by demanding loyalty, not to a people, but merely to a single person. In nineteenth-century Austria the principle was neither exclusive nor totalitarian, making no demands for religious, linguistic, or social uniformity. It did not divide humanity into majorities and minorities and was satisfied with the loyalty of the individual. Throughout the centuries the Habsburgs broadened their appeal by refusing to identify themselves with any one nationality. At various times they spoke Spanish and French as well as German.

The character, personality, and ability of the next to the last ruling Habsburg are disputed. During Franz Joseph's lifetime, and as late as the Second World War, many writers were critical, emphasizing his intellectual mediocrity and lack of ideas and imagination. They were indignant over his absorption in details and his unwillingness to introduce radical constitutional reforms after 1871. These judgments have not been entirely abandoned; but more recently historians have stressed the ruler's high sense of honor, impartiality, and gentlemanliness. All who met the Emperor-King were especially impressed by his awe-inspiring majesty.

Franz Joseph has also been accused, and not altogether inaccurately, of being "essentially medieval." The Emperor's aversion to all things modern was proverbial. He refused to use telephones or elevators and insisted that state documents intended for his eyes be handwritten. Only rarely did he set foot in an automobile, although he did not object to using the telegraph and railroad, inventions of his youth. His dislike for the modern theory of popular sovereignty was already clearly revealed during the Revolutions of 1848. His faith in the divine right of monarchs far into the twentieth century was equally old-fashioned. Yet it was this same faith that convinced him of his deep responsibility to God.

Reversing the usual pattern, Franz Joseph began his reign as something of a tyrant when he abolished the Kremsier Parliament and brutally suppressed the Hungarian rebellion. His devotion to duty, however, and his endurance in the face of personal tragedy (his son, Rudolf, committed suicide; his wife, Elizabeth, was murdered by an Italian anarchist; and his nephew, Franz Ferdinand, was assassinated by a Pan-Serb fanatic) eventually won him nearly universal respect and even the love of his people. In his old age he became a grandfather figure. Sons rebel against their fathers, but toward their grandfathers they are more likely to be sentimental.

The Viennese affectionately referred to Franz Joseph as "our Emperor" (something few Berliners would say about Kaiser Wilhelm II). His "affair" (if it can be called that) with the actress Frau Katherine Schratt only endeared him to his subjects by making him seem more human. He loved the atmosphere of Frau Schratt's home, her coffee cake, comfortable chairs, and Viennese gossip. His letters to her, published after her death in 1940, reveal a warm sense of humor and an ability to look at himself critically.

Centripetal Forces in the Dual Monarchy

Of the many centripetal forces in the Monarchy other than the dynasty, geography and economic developments played important, but not unequivocal, roles. Austria-Hungary in 1914 contained a little more than 53 million people in 264,204 square miles, an area only slightly smaller than the state of Texas. In size it ranked second in Europe; in population it was third. Almost every type of climate and topography could be found within its borders, from the Adriatic coast with its Mediterranean climate to the severe Continental weather of Galicia, and from the rugged Alps of Tyrol to the flat and fertile Hungarian plain. This geographic variety was naturally conducive to a wide range of agricultural and manufactured products, and therefore to a certain interdependency of the Monarchy's provinces.

Some writers have noted that the Austrian half of the Monarchy, by itself, was a geographic oddity, forming an elongated semicircle divided by numerous mountain ranges. With Hungary, however, it formed a compact territory blessed with a large market and enough mineral wealth to facilitate a substantial degree of industrialization. Austria's industry, in turn, was balanced by the agricultural wealth of Hungary.

Thanks to the Monarchy's natural resources and sizable foreign investments, the number of factories in Austria-Hungary in the period 1903–1913 increased by 40.6 percent, while real income rose by 59 percent in Austria and 75 percent in Hungary, a more rapid rate of growth than in either Great Britain or Germany during the same period. This bounty was shared almost equally by all nationalities and classes in the Monarchy.

Prosperity in Austria-Hungary should not, of course, be exaggerated. Nearly half the Hungarian population on the eve of the First World War was still impoverished. Unskilled labor in Austria was badly paid, and there was an unfavorable balance of trade between Austria-Hungary and the outside world as well as growing economic friction between the two halves of the Monarchy as the Hungarians attempted to develop their own industries. Austrian state finances were deteriorating in 1913 due to greatly enlarged military appropriations, and recurrent deficits occurred in the state railways. Industrial development in parts of Austria and most of Hungary was hurt by the backward state of agricultural techniques which reduced possible exports and the size of the consuming market. In short, Austria-Hungary was a typical developing state in 1914, still backward in many respects, but having great potential. To many Habsburg subjects general well-being seemed just around the corner.

The civil services of Austria and Hungary and the common Austro-Hungarian army and navy are also included among the forces binding together the Danube Monarchy. Austrian, but not Hungarian, society could be considered democratic, since even the highest offices in the Imperial service, both civil and military, were open to talent regardless of nationality or social background. To be sure, the more prestigious positions were held by German-speaking Austrians, but this was a matter of expedience, not deliberate discrimination. At the lower echelons of public life—in the teaching profession, for instance—the smaller nationalities were generally represented in proportion to their numbers.

The efficiency and honesty of the civil service have been almost unanimously praised. Compared with that of Tsarist Russia and the Balkans, or of the postwar Successor States, the Austro-Hungarian record is especially impressive. Austrian bureaucrats did have a tendency to be servile toward superiors and haughty toward the public (attitudes which many have retained to this day), but this did not prevent fair treatment. Even the police served the public well. The British journalist Henry Wickham Steed acknowledged that "the readiness with which the lower classes appeal to the police is remarkable and indicates the success of the authorities to make the common people feel that the State is on their side."[6]

The armed forces of the Dual Monarchy were equally *Kaisertreu* (loyal to the emperors) and, unlike the German army, were relatively free of class prejudice. The mere existence of the army and navy was itself a remarkable fact, composed as they were of members of all Habsburg nationalities. They not only defended the dual state, but also had a civilizing influence on recruits from the less developed nationalities. Besides being taught to shoot and ride, the raw army recruit learned reading, writing, arithmetic, and history as well as the duties and rights of a citizen. The more intelligent were instructed in scouting,

[6] *The Hapsburg Monarchy,* 2d ed. (New York: Scribner's, 1913), p. 96.

reading maps, and surveying. Their elementary "army German" was, of course, serviceable throughout Central and East Central Europe long after their military days were over.

Cultural forms have not always been included among the Monarchy's cohesive forces but deserve to be. If there was no sense of common statehood among Habsburg subjects, there was to a considerable extent at least a common life style throughout both halves of the empire. Members of the middle and upper classes in the larger towns and cities ate many of the same dishes, listened to the same music, lived and worked in buildings of similar architectural design, and to a considerable extent even read the same German-language newspapers and periodicals. Vienna was the cultural capital for the whole Habsburg realm as well as for southeastern Europe. Many of the best minds in music, medicine, and German drama were attracted to the Danube metropolis, whose population surpassed two million in 1910.

The people of Austria-Hungary also tended to share the same outlook on life. Skeptical, almost fatalistic, they were self-critical and able to face adversity with relative equanimity. They preferred the sensuous, pragmatic, and convenient to things showy, impressive, or philosophical.

The pessimistic works of Viennese writers around the turn of the twentieth century have been held up by some critics as proof that sensitive Austrians realized the Monarchy was doomed. More likely, liberal Jewish authors like Arthur Schnitzler and Hugo von Hofmannsthal were simply depressed by the triumph of Christian Socialism in Vienna with its anti-Semitism, clericalism, and municipal socialism, things anathema to classical liberals everywhere.

But Christian Socialism was hardly a threat to the Monarchy. On the contrary, along with Social Democracy, it became one of the two great movements of Austrian revival in the latter part of the nineteenth century. Both parties rejected nationalism, favoring instead the international ties of Catholicism and the industrial working class respectively. The Roman Catholic Church had been historically a staunch supporter of the Habsburgs, and Marxian Socialists supported the Dual Monarchy because of the advantages in the Monarchy's economic expansion.

Although the Christian Social and the Social Democratic parties became the two largest in the Reichsrat following the suffrage reform, neither was entirely successful in appealing to non-German nationalities. Christian Socialism spread only to the already loyal Slovene areas, and Czech Socialists broke off from the parent organization in 1907. The value of the two parties to the state, moreover, was partially canceled out by their mutual antipathy.

Plans for Federalization

Despite the Monarchy's many centripetal forces, there remained the problem of nationalism and its demand for national autonomy. To many critics, both before and after the First World War, the solution was deceptively easy: federalization on the basis of self-governing national territories would have fulfilled national ambitions and guaranteed the Monarchy's survival. Such a plan, however, ignored a host of difficulties. Austria-Hungary consisted of at least eleven enormously dissimilar nationalities. Some of them, notably the Slovaks and Ruthenes, were far too backward for self-government, as was demonstrated after 1918. In few places could the nationalities be readily divided without leaving large minorities on either side of a new border. What ethnic lines there were seldom coincided with historic, geographic, or economic boundaries.

To have federalized Austria-Hungary on an ethnic basis would have required the destruction of the ancient Austrian crownlands and the historic boundaries of Hungary. Although these historic units were rarely homogeneous ethnically, they often made good geographic and economic sense, and retained a strong appeal to the traditionalist peasants. Their destruction was made all the more difficult by local majority nationalities insisting on the maintenance of the province's "historic unity." The Czechs in Bohemia, the Poles in Galicia, and the Germans in Carinthia and Styria fell into this category. If a nationality found itself a crownland minority, it demanded "ethnic rights," as did the Germans in Bohemia and Moravia, the Ruthenes of Galicia, and some Slovenes in Carinthia and Styria. Thus, no matter which solution was envisaged—crownland autonomy or ethnic autonomy—almost as many people were bound to be enraged as satisfied.

Those who decry the Habsburgs' failure to federalize the Monarchy forget that it was precisely in those territories where local autonomy already existed, as in Hungary and Galicia, that discrimination against national minorities was greatest; wherever the Vienna government still maintained some power, national oppression was held in check.

Even if the nationalities could have agreed on the boundaries of autonomous states, serious problems would have remained. It was already difficult for representatives of Austria and Hungary to agree on common appropriations. If the Habsburg Monarchy had consisted of not two but eleven states, conflicts would have been multiplied many times over.

Franz Joseph was cold to the idea of federalization, fearing it would weaken the power of the Monarchy and facilitate outright secession. It might also increase the ambition of Italy, Serbia, Rumania, and Russia to "liberate" their brethren. The Emperor-King therefore, was not simply being a "hidebound reactionary" in preferring no medication at all to the risks involved in major surgery.

Federalization in the Austrian part of the Monarchy would have run also into outside resistance. The Magyars could legitimately claim that it violated the terms of the Compromise. The deathbed attempt to federalize Austria in October 1918 did, in fact, provoke the Magyars into renouncing the *Ausgleich*. The government of the German Empire also felt it had a vested interest in the Austro-Hungarian *status quo,* as any change in the internal balance of power might endanger the Austro-German military alliance of 1879.

A more modest plan for national reform than federalism was "Trialism," which foresaw the creation of a third state consisting of the Habsburg South Slavs: Croats, Serbs, and possibly the Slovenes. Trialism won the backing of nearly all the Croatians and many of the Serbs in the Monarchy. Vienna was also willing to support it provided that the Slovene districts, vital for Austrian access to the Adriatic, were not included. Only the Magyars were adamant, seeing in a triple state a diminution of their influence in common affairs. Even with Hungary's consent it is unlikely that Trialism would have proved a permanent solution to the nationality problem; Czech ambitions in particular would have been aroused. It is hard to see how there could have been a compromise between dualism and complete federalism.

No constitutional changes were made or even attempted on an empire-wide scale in Austria-Hungary in the last decades of the Monarchy's existence, but a number of constitutional reforms were carried out in individual Austrian crownlands. The German-Czech dispute in Moravia was settled by the Compromise of 1905 which divided the province into national districts. Bohemian Czechs denounced the Compromise as a sellout, but the Moravian nationalities, being less concerned about historic rights, were satisfied. A similar settlement with equally happy results was reached in 1911 in the remote easternmost province of Bucovina.

Still another national quarrel was resolved when the Poles and Ruthenes of Galicia reached an understanding in February 1914. The Ruthenes had doubled their representation in the Reichsrat in the franchise reform of 1907, and in 1914 their ratio of seats in the Galician diet was set at 27 percent. This figure was still low compared to their 42 percent of the province's total population, but it was high enough to break the Poles' earlier political monopoly. The Poles' control of educational and cultural institutions was brought to an end by the agreement. The compromise evoked great optimism that a turning point had been reached in the relations between the two rivals. With the settlement of the Galician question only the Bohemian problem, of the major Austrian national disputes, had not yet been adjudicated.

The Balance Sheet in 1914

The picture of Austria-Hungary on the eve of the First World War is obviously complex. Those observers who have looked only at the darker side have had no trouble in persuading themselves that Austria-Hungary was doomed, with or without a war. In their view the lesser nationalities were all determined to free themselves from "the yoke of Habsburg oppression" and were merely biding their time until the proper moment arrived to establish complete independence. Pro-Habsburg writers insist that the Monarchy was basically sound and was endangered only by a handful of traitors and greedy neighbors. Both interpretations are misleading. Many Bohemian Czechs and Serbs, some Croats, extreme Magyar nationalists, Transylvanian Rumanians, and a good many Austro-Italians were unappeased. The German Austrians, Poles, Ruthenes, Slovaks, and most Magyars, Slovenes, and Rumanians were reasonably content. Only a smattering of radicals, found for the most part among Austro-Italian and Serbian intellectuals, strove for complete dismemberment of the Dual Monarchy. Other nationalities, although having grievances, sought constitutional alterations within the framework of the state. Unfortunately their extreme demands were irreconcilable. But local settlements in Moravia, Bucovina, and Galicia, as well as improving Magyar-Croat relations, showed that the nationality struggle was not insoluble.

Some oppression did exist in Austria-Hungry, but with the partial exception of Hungary, it was mainly psychological. There was a trend toward equality in both halves of the Monarchy, even if along completely different lines. In Austria the principle of national equality was carried further than in any other European country except Switzerland. Every nationality enjoyed full civil and cultural rights and had political influence corresponding roughly to its relative size. In Hungary a kind of equality was being achieved through Magyarization.

Only one domestic issue existed which could prove a mortal danger to the integrity of the Monarchy in the foreseeable future: Magyar nationalism. Other national ambitions might have become deadly at some later date, but dissatisfied nationalities in 1914 were still too weak and divided seriously to challenge the Habsburgs. Furthermore, the two most vital elements in the preservation of the state—the civil and military services—while not entirely unaffected by nationalism, remained trustworthy.

Although around the turn of the century there had been much speculation both inside Austria-Hungary and abroad concerning the Dual Monarchy's impending demise, such talk was heard less frequently in 1914. Clearly there was sufficient combustible material in the Monarchy for an explosion, but the ignition would have to come from the outside.

CHAPTER TWO

War and Dissolution

Austria-Hungary and the Balkans, 1878–1914

Throughout the nineteenth and into the twentieth century, the Dual Monarchy was largely terra incognita to the outside world. Of those Americans and Britons touring the Continent, for example, barely 1 or 2 percent took the trouble to visit the Monarchy. Diplomats, however, viewed the Habsburg state as an essential part of the European balance of power and feared that its disappearance would lead to a scramble for territory. Western capitals appreciated the Monarchy's maintenance of law and order in an otherwise lawless part of Europe while serving as a useful counterpoise to both German and Russian imperialism. Conservatives and most political leaders in the West were unconcerned about Austria-Hungary's multinational character and neither group showed much interest in the Monarchy's individual nationalities. Around the turn of the century a sprinkling of liberal intellectuals, such as Louis Eisemann in France and Wickham Steed and Robert W. Seton-Watson in Great Britain, began to express a sympathetic concern for the "submerged" nationalities and proposed various changes to satisfy their grievances; but even these writers did not foresee, let alone desire, the dissolution of the Empire, and in any case they had little practical influence.

Knowledge and suspicion of Austria-Hungary increased abroad in 1878-1879 when Austria occupied the Turkish provinces of Bosnia and Herzegovina and concluded a military alliance with Germany. The occupation was principally the result of Franz Joseph's anxiety to find territorial compensation for the loss of his Italian possessions and to forestall any occupation of the provinces by Serbia or Montenegro. Austrian Dalmatia, moreover, would be more secure if its hinterland belonged to the Monarchy. Russian and Turkish opposition abroad and the antipathy of the German Liberal party at home convinced the overly cautious Austro-Hungarian foreign minister, Count Gyula Andrássy, to substitute military occupation and administration for outright annexation of the provinces. In this unsettled issue lay one of the basic causes for the outbreak of the First World War.

Bosnia-Herzegovina was to Austria-Hungary what Alsace-Lorraine was to Germany. The occupation of the provinces embittered the neighbors of both countries: Serbia and Russia in the case of Austria, France in the case of Germany. Finding themselves in similar circumstances, Austria and Germany concluded a defensive alliance in 1879.

The new partnership pleased those Austrians who had not yet recovered from the shock of being expelled from Germany in 1866; it was welcomed by Magyars as a means of maintaining the domestic *status quo*. Militarily it was vital for protection against Russia along Austria's exposed Galician frontier. In other respects, however, the alliance was a mistake. The Austro-Slavs (Czechs, Slovaks, Slovenes, Croatians, Poles, and Ruthenes), many of whom were pro-Russian, resented the alliance's Russophobe character. It rendered Austria-Hungary suspect in the eyes of the Western Powers (with whom Austria had no real conflict of interest) as an accomplice of an aggressive German Reich. Ideally, the multinational empire should have remained neutral like multinational Switzerland. But unlike the Swiss Republic, Austria's imperialistic neighbors would not leave the Monarchy in peace (or in one piece).

In 1882 the Dual Alliance was converted into the Triple Alliance to include Italy, irate over the recent French occupation of Tunisia. The association of Austria and Italy in the same alliance system proved highly artificial. The Italians could never sincerely renounce their claim to fellow Italian-speakers in southern Austria, and Vienna could never compromise its territorial integrity. The two countries, moreover, were at odds over who should control Montenegro and Albania. Once Franco-Italian relations were patched up in 1902 the Triple Alliance became little more than a scrap of paper, even though Italy remained a nominal member until 1915. Serbia allied with Germany in 1881, and Rumania was secretly added to the German alliance network two years later; but the Balkan additions were even less valuable than Italy. They too eventually backed out of their commitments at critical moments.

Austrian security was temporarily enhanced by a "gentlemen's agreement" with Russia in 1897 thereby putting the Balkan question "on ice" for more than a decade while the Russians were busy in the Far East. The understanding left the western half of the peninsula as Austria's sphere of influence, while the eastern half fell to Russia. But no one bothered to consult the wishes of those most immediately concerned, namely the Serbs and Bulgarians. Serbia was alienated from Austria by the commercial conflict known as the "Pig War" (1903–1906), which induced Belgrade to escape economic servitude by seeking Russia's protection just when Russian expansionism in the Orient had been halted by the Japanese. Renewed Tsarist interest in the Balkans brought the Austro-Russian rapproachement to a sudden end in 1908.

The occasion was the Austrian annexation of Bosnia-

Herzegovina. For all practical purposes the provinces were already integral parts of the Habsburg Monarchy. They were included in the Austro-Hungarian customs union; their people carried Austro-Hungarian passports and served in the Habsburg armed services. To give up the provinces was unthinkable. Yet this was precisely what the "Young Turks" who seized power in Constantinople in July 1908 demanded.

The Austro-Hungarian foreign minister, Baron Lexa von Aehrenthal, was placed in a delicate situation by the Turkish Revolution. Surrender of Bosnia-Herzegovina was out of the question, but maintenance of the *status quo* would leave Turkish and Serbian aspirations undiminished. The only alternative seemed to be full annexation. In Aehrenthal's thinking this would have a calming effect on the Balkans by creating a sense of permanency. At the same time it would show Europe and the restless nationalities of the Monarchy that Austria-Hungary was still a great power. Germany would likewise be forced to realize that Austria was capable of pursuing an independent foreign policy.

The Russian foreign minister, A. P. Izvolski, conveniently offered (under mysterious circumstances) to support Aehrenthal in exchange for Austrian favors in the traditional Russian goal of controlling the Turkish Straits. Austria proceeded with the annexation within a month, but Izvolski, professing to be surprised by the swiftness of this move, was unable to gain British and French approval for his half of the bargain. He felt double-crossed at having been left in the embarrassing position of having given something away for nothing. Turks and Serbs were enraged by the annexation, and the Italians cried foul at having been given no compensation. Even the Germans, learning of the Austrian action only at the last minute, were not exactly delighted. St. Petersburg considered war, but thought better of it when Berlin gave Vienna firm support rather than lose its one remaining dependable ally.

The aftermath of the annexation must have shocked Aehrenthal. Instead of German apron strings being cut, they were tightened. Increasingly apprehensive about the possibility of war, the Austro-Hungarian and German chiefs of staff inaugurated a correspondence fostering the conviction in Vienna that it could count on German support in case of war with Serbia and Russia. The Austro-Russian "entente," needless to say, was now dead and Pan-Serb and Pan-Italian pretensions were soaring. The British and French, although refusing to snatch Russia's chestnuts from its self-made fire, also grew cooler toward the Habsburg Monarchy, which to them seemed to be assuming the status of a German satellite. The reaction within Austria-Hungary, to be sure, was favorable: Magyars and German Austrians were pleased with the Monarchy's audacity, and Slavs welcomed the addition of kinfolk to the south. The annexation also gave every indication of being the first step in the creation of a Habsburg South Slav state. Domestic gains, however, were more than offset by the diplomatic losses occasioned by the crisis.

Austria's international situation deteriorated still further as a result of the Balkan Wars of 1912–1913 fought over the spoils of the Ottoman Empire. Turkey in the first war, and Bulgaria in the second were the losers; Serbia and Rumania the biggest winners. The victors' appetite for territorial aggrandizement now grew with the eating; the next meal would logically be Austria-Hungary. In these designs they enjoyed the encouragement of Russia, still seeking revenge for its humiliation over Bosnia.

Austria's diplomatic posture in 1914 was not enviable, but neither was it as hopeless as some Austrian statesmen imagined. The Monarchy had succeeded in expelling Serbian troops from the Adriatic coast after the end of the Second Balkan War and had been instrumental in setting up an independent Albania, both moves being accompanied by the diplomatic backing of Berlin. Bulgaria, smarting from its defeat and loss of Macedonia to Serbia, was anxious for an alliance with the Dual Monarchy. Only the pro-Rumanian attitude of the German emperor, Wilhelm II, and the Habsburg heir apparent, Franz Ferdinand, stood in the path of its conclusion. The Ottoman Empire was also anxious to align itself with the Central Powers; the makings existed for a new balance of power in the Balkans that might have restrained Serbia and Rumania.

The Sarajevo Assassination

Both Bulgaria and Turkey were soon drawn into the Austro-German orbit, but only after the outbreak of war. The immediate cause of the conflict was the assassination of Archduke Franz Ferdinand.

The Habsburg archduke was a remarkably enigmatic figure. Cold and aloof, he had few intimates and did not seek them. The only pleasures he allowed himself were his wife and children, his rose garden, and hunting. (He could reputedly "trim" a hedge with a gun at a great distance.) He has been credited with the plans and ability to rejuvenate the Monarchy, but also with a character and personality that could wreck it. He was exceptionally well aware of the central problems of the Monarchy, both foreign and domestic. The Magyars, for example, he recognized as potentially the most disruptive nationality in the Dual Monarchy, and he held them responsible for spreading chauvinism to other ethnic groups. The common denominator of his many reform projects was the reduction of Magyar domination over the minorities of Hungary as well as the limitation of Magyar influence in joint imperial affairs. Franz Ferdinand, we can safely assume, was not a popular figure in Magyar society.

The heir apparent also recognized the urgency of settling the South Slav question and was commonly thought to favor "Trialism"; his distrust of Serbs and Croats, however, led him to abandon this scheme long before he made his fateful trip to Sarajevo. His last idea of constitutional reform favored federalism, but with the retention of the old Austrian crownlands, along with increased power for the central government in Vienna. Paradoxically he had the ideas and the energy to at least attempt great reforms, but not the experience or personality. By contrast, Franz Joseph had great experience, but no new ideas and little energy.

In international relations Franz Ferdinand consistently opposed preventative war against Serbia, since it would in all probability lead to war with Russia. An Austro-Russian war was his nightmare; it would destroy both empires and with them the monarchical principle.

The archduke and his wife were murdered on June 28, 1914, in Sarajevo, the Bosnian capital (a murder he had predicted to his nephew Karl, the future emperor, nearly two months before). Franz Ferdinand had been attending maneuvers of the Austro-Hungarian army; unofficially, the purpose of the visit was to fortify dynastic loyalty in the recently annexed provinces and to offset revolutionary Pan-Serb agitation.

Most of the details of the plot and assassination are by now fairly well known (see Joachim Remak's *The Origins of World War I,* also in the Berkshire Studies in European History). It is reasonably clear that the plot was organized by the Chief of Intelligence of the Serbian army, Colonel Dragutin Dimitrijević. Other members of the Serbian government knew of the plot one month before it was carried out, but did not effectively warn the Austrian government or prevent the assassins from carrying out their work. We know too that the Serbian government did everything in its power to hide its responsibility while publicly professing its innocence.

Although Franz Ferdinand was unloved in Austria-Hungary, loyalists who wanted the Monarchy reformed had placed their hopes in him. His murder created widespread and genuine anger, particularly since it was the seventh attempt in four years by Bosnian youths with Belgrade connections to assassinate Habsburg officials. That Austro-Hungarian authorities would put an end to these Pan-Serb outrages once and for all was taken for granted throughout the Monarchy; a passive attitude by Vienna would have gravely lowered Austria-Hungary's prestige both at home and abroad.

The most auspicious time for action was during the first few days following the murder, while horrified world reaction favored Austria and held Belgrade responsible. However, nearly four weeks passed before an Austro-Hungarian ultimatum was delivered. During the long interval a leisurely investigation of the plot was begun by the Sarajevo police. A report by a Viennese investigator dated July 13 proved that the conspiracy had originated in Belgrade but did not accuse the Serbian government of foreknowledge. The Austro-Hungarian Foreign Ministry prepared a dossier on the crime for the benefit of foreign capitals, but the document was not released until after the publication of the Austrian ultimatum, too late to affect the course of events.

In the meantime, pressure for swift and drastic action was mounting. Von Schierbrand, who was an eyewitness, describes how

> . . . Everywhere the easygoing Viennese were brought up to the pitch of martial furor. The old songs of Austria's former glory . . . burst forth and were heard everywhere. . . . Everybody rose, old and young . . . and while they sang tears of emotion glistened in their eyes. Never before had I seen a people in such a delirium of wrath.[1]

In Berlin, initial words of caution were contradicted by Wilhelm, who urged the Austrians to strike quickly against Serbia while world public opinion was still on their side. The German ambassador in Vienna also hinted darkly that his country would seek allies elsewhere if the Monarchy made only a tepid response to the Serbian challenge. Should Russia intervene, Austria-Hungary could count on German support. This was the famous (or notorious) "blank check."

It was the misfortune of the Habsburg Monarchy to have as its foreign minister a man of the caliber of Count Leopold von Berchtold. Charming and pleasant-mannered, he took pride in being the best-dressed man in the Monarchy. Unfortunately, he gave every appearance of being shy, nervous, and unsure of himself (although he had served with distinction as ambassador to Russia before his appointment as head of the Austro-Hungarian Foreign Ministry). Usually vacillating and indecisive, Berchtold had scored a diplomatic triumph over Serbia the previous autumn by helping to establish the independence of Albania, thus denying Serbia access to the Adriatic. The temptation for a repeat performance must have been irresistible. He was strengthened in his urge to teach the Serbians a lesson by Franz

---

[1] Wolf von Schierbrand, *Austria-Hungary, The Polyglot Empire* (New York: Frederick A. Stokes, 1917), p. 187.

Conrad von Hötzendorf, the Austro-Hungarian chief of staff. Conrad was bitter that accounts with Serbia had not been settled the year before, a view shared by his German counterpart. In the past, Franz Ferdinand had always restrained Conrad's eagerness for a preventative war. But now the heir apparent was no longer on the scene.

When Berchtold learned that he could rely on unconditional German support, the only obstacle to war was the prime minister of Hungary, Count István Tisza. Tisza's first impulse was flatly to oppose war, partly out of pacifist scruples, but mainly because he dreaded the consequences for Hungary of even a victorious conflict. If Russia intervened and won, Hungary would be partitioned. If Serbia were crushed, Austria's relative position in the Monarchy might be improved, and Hungary would then be relegated to the status of an Austrian crownland. The risk of facing Russia and Rumania without German support, however, finally swung him over to the war party, but only on the condition that should war and the conquest of Serbia ensue, nothing more than "frontier rectifications" would be taken by the Monarchy. Tisza's stipulation made the worst of two possible worlds. It failed to avoid war and it prevented the formation of a South Slav state within the Monarchy, the one thing that might have given the war meaning.

The Austrian ultimatum with a forty-eight hour time limit was delivered to Serbia on July 23 under circumstances far less favorable than those existing a few weeks earlier. Foreign interest in the assassination had by now largely disappeared. To make matters worse, the Austro-Hungarian Foreign Ministry had given the impression that its note to Serbia would not be extreme and at Berlin's suggestion, had delayed sending it until an official French visit to St. Petersburg was terminated. The timing of the ultimatum as well as its severity aroused immediate suspicion in foreign capitals. Berchtold purposely wrote it in such a way that its acceptance was next to impossible. It demanded that Serbia punish the conspirators, prevent future anti-Austrian propaganda, and accept Austro-Hungarian assistance in suppressing secret anti-Austrian societies within Serbia. The charges it leveled against Serbia were actually an understatement of that country's real responsibility, but they went beyond what the Austrians could prove at the time. Nevertheless, the Serbian government actually considered accepting the ultimatum, even though that step would have meant an unmitigated humiliation and possibly revolution. The hesitation, however, was short-lived, as the Russians hastened to assure their protégés of their unqualified support. Now it was St. Petersburg's turn to issue a blank check.

Belgrade knew that any reply short of unconditional agreement would be rejected by Vienna. Therefore, in order to gain international sympathy, it made its response as conciliatory as possible. Five demands were accepted outright, four conditionally, and only one rejected. From the Austrian point of view the reply was nevertheless wholly inadequate, and the Austro-Hungarian minister in Belgrade returned to Vienna at once. Serbia prohibited an Austro-Hungarian investigation of the crime and offered no guarantee that future propaganda against the Monarchy would cease, the two most essential aspects of the ultimatum. All the same, the ploy worked. Serbia appeared reasonable and accommodating. Austria was now the intransigent bully.

Austria declared war against Serbia on July 28; two days later the Russians reacted with a general mobilization, knowing full well that the move signified the start of a major European war. Austria-Hungary had mobilized only along its frontier with Serbia; it went to war to protect its territorial integrity against the challenge of Pan-Serbism. Russia, unthreatened, went to war merely to maintain its prestige and influence in the Balkans. The Habsburg Monarchy did not object to Russian control of the Straits or predominance in the eastern Balkans, but it did oppose Russian support of Serbian (and also Rumanian) territorial ambitions.

Austro-Hungarian policy was equally unrealistic in the hectic July days of 1914. Austria's determination to crush Serbia militarily could serve no useful purpose, even had it not led to Russian intervention and a European war. Military defeat would have left the Serbs and Russians fanatically committed to revenge. The Triple Entente of Russia, France, and Britain would have been consolidated and Italy further alienated from the

Triple Alliance. Austria's impatience with Serbia is easily understood; it is not so easy to comprehend the Austrian expectation
that war itself could cure the Monarchy's domestic troubles.
At best they could only be postponed. Austro-Hungarian statesmen evidently exaggerated the double peril of the domestic
crisis and the Serbian challenge and in the process lost their
poise and good sense. In their partial defense, however, it
should be noted that their nervousness might not have been
nearly so extreme had the Russians not backed Serbian and
Rumanian irredentism. If the Austrians acted with recklessness
in the crisis, the Russians and Serbs displayed little more
moderation.

From the Commencement of Hostilities to the Death of Franz Joseph

The First World War had a peculiar beginning. Austria-
Hungary was the first state to declare war. The Austro-Serb
conflict then developed into a European war by virtue of Russia's
resolution to prevent the subjugation of Serbia and Germany's
equal determination to stand behind its ally. Actual fighting,
however, first occurred in Western Europe. The reason was
Germany's so-called Schlieffen Plan, which envisaged the invasion and defeat of France before Russia could complete its
mobilization in the estimated time of six weeks. The Plan was
catastrophic for Germany, as it failed to eliminate France and
provoked British intervention. Not so well known are the even
more ruinous consequences for Austria. When Russia mobilized
in half the time expected, the Austro-Hungarian army, whose
contingency war plans had been poorly coordinated with those
of Germany, was forced to hold off most of the Tsarist forces
single-handedly while the Germans were engaged in the West.
More damaging yet to Austria-Hungary was the stationing of
only a fraction of its men along the Austro-Russian border.
Conrad von Hötzendorf had been convinced he could deal first
with Serbia, then with Russia. Even when he realized his mistake he redeployed only about half the army to the north and
then launched an offensive before the transfer had been com-

pleted. The divided forces were hurled back on both fronts. In the first month of the fighting Austria-Hungary lost one-third of its original army including its best officers; 250,000 men were dead or wounded, and 100,000 more were taken prisoner. The deterioration of morale in the Monarchy caused by these disasters was never fully ameliorated.

The bankruptcy of both the Schlieffen Plan and Conrad von Hötzendorf's tactics meant that the war would be a long one, something almost no one had anticipated and which Austria, with its delicate internal balance, could least afford. The prolongation of the fighting gave the two natural enemies of the Habsburg Monarchy, Italy and Rumania, an opportunity to intervene and stake out claims to Austro-Hungarian territory. The Schlieffen Plan negated the value of the German alliance for Austria by neglecting to provide sufficient protection against Russia. For Germany it was one step on the road to military defeat; for Austria-Hungary it paved the way to absolute political destruction.

Even when it became apparent that the war would not end soon, nearly all Habsburg nationalities supported the Austro-Hungarian cause and did so with considerable enthusiasm. There were some exceptions: Many Serbs identified themselves with their nationality, not their state; at the start of the war many Ruthenes in eastern Galicia welcomed the invading Tsarist armies, although a few months of Russification cured most of them of their Russophilia.

A great deal of attention during and after the war has been given to Czech desertions; a fair number of Czech soldiers did go over to the enemy side, but in comparison to the number of Czechs in uniform the percentage was small and did not affect the conduct of the war until its later stages. Some 5000 Czech civilians were condemned by courts-martial, and another 20,000 were imprisoned; but there were also signs of Czech satisfaction over Habsburg victories. Probably most Czechs passionately favored neither alliance, but simply took a pragmatic "wait and see" attitude. Some hoped for a Russian victory; others were pro-West. As long as the war went well for the Central Powers, symptoms of disaffection were few. With three irons in the fire the Czechs would be on the side of the victors no matter who won.

The intervention of Italy and Rumania in 1915 and 1916 was an enormous factor in the maintenance of Habsburg loyalism. It was scarcely surprising that these two German allies refused to enter the war in 1914 on the side of the Central Powers; it would have been completely contrary to their interests to do so. There was also nothing extraordinary about both countries attempting to sell their neutrality to the highest bidder. What is astonishing in the Italian case is the refusal of a generous offer of Austro-Italian territory in exchange for mere neutrality. Instead, Rome took an imperialistic bribe from the Triple Entente which required intervention.

More specifically, the Austrians, at Germany's urging, agreed to the immediate cession of the purely Italian-speaking Trentino, with its 300,000 inhabitants, together with a small strip of land west of the Isonzo River. Trieste would become a free city, and Italy would get the Albanian port of Valona. The fate of other Austrian areas would be negotiated after the war. In short, the Austrians conceded to Italy virtually everything the latter could absorb without creating a new irredentist problem or damaging the economy of the annexed areas. Although the offer was rejected, it remained of more than academic interest. Once declined, it necessitated an imperialistic policy by the Italian government. No ministry could afford a peace that did not go far beyond the Austrian concession if intervention was to seem worthwhile to the Italian people.

The Triple Entente could easily outbid the Central Powers by offering territories other than its own. In the secret Treaty of London, concluded on April 26, 1915, Britain, France, and Russia agreed to Italian demands which included not only all 768,000 Italian-speaking Austrians, but well over one million non-Italians. Most of the Adriatic islands were to become Italian as well as the northern part of Dalmatia, both overwhelmingly Croatian. In an attempt to spread discord between the two halves of the Monarchy, Rome excluded the Hungarian coastline in Croatia from its list of territorial demands.

A good deal of nonsense has been written about the London accord; it has been denounced as a cynical piece of Machiavellian imperialism by Italy and the principal roadblock to a separate peace with Austria-Hungary. Cynical it may have been, but it was no more imperialistic than many other wartime and postwar treaties. It is most unlikely that the treaty prevented the Dual Monarchy from signing a separate peace, as there was almost no prospect for such a peace under any circumstances. It did not even make the future existence of the Habsburg Monarchy impossible, as many writers have maintained. The Monarchy would have retained an outlet to the Adriatic and in any case already did more trading from the Elbe riverport of Aussig in northern Bohemia than from its much more famous seaport of Trieste. The treaty in fact assumed that Austria-Hungary would remain a great power after the war, albeit somewhat reduced in size.

The London agreement can be condemned most readily, not so much for its cynicism or immorality, as for its stupidity. Even had the war ended within the six months estimated by Rome, with Austria still extant, the treaty would have been a calamity for Italy. Pan-Serb passions would have been deflected from Austria to Italy, and the Habsburg South Slav nationalists would have been driven into the Austrian camp. Constant military preparedness would have been needed for Italy to retain its precarious hold on the eastern Adriatic; the only alternative would have been a new alliance with Austria. For the Habsburg Monarchy the treaty would have meant increased commercial dependence on Germany, a condition hardly beneficial to the Entente.

Not only did Italy's intervention fail to end the war in six months, it did not even prevent the conquest of Serbia, Montenegro, and Russian Poland by Austro-German arms in 1915. Italy's betrayal of the Triple Alliance rallied the Austro-Hungarian nationalities behind the Habsburg banner, especially when fairly accurate news of the treaty became widely known. The final irony was that the intervention cost Italy nearly as many lives (600,000) as there were Austro-Italians liberated.

The intervention of Rumania in 1916 proved equally useful to the Central Powers. The Regat was overrun in a matter of weeks, leaving its valuable wheat fields and oil wells at the disposal of Germany and Austria-Hungary for the remainder of the war. And once more, sagging Austro-Hungarian morale was given a lift.

With Rumania's defeat at the end of 1916 all major Habsburg objectives had been reached. Serbia, the original antagonist, had been beaten and occupied, as had been Rumania. Italy and Russia were on the defensive and no longer constituted a real danger. One thing stood in the way of peace: German imperialism. Although the Schlieffen Plan had not brought the expected quick end of the war, it did result in huge tracts of French soil being occupied by the German army. As the year 1916 began, Germany was in possession also of great expanses of Russian territory. Too much land had been conquered for a compromise peace and too little for an imposed German settlement. The German ruling class (Junkers, industrialists, and military leaders) feared that anything short of an annexationist peace would undermine its prestige and set the stage for social revolution. Austro-Hungarian statesmen, on the other hand, feared that prolongation of the war for the sake of German imperialism would incite national revolutions. German and Austro-Hungarian war aims were therefore completely incompatible: German leaders preferred a long war to a cheap peace; Habsburg leaders preferred a cheap peace to a long war.

Only a public facade of harmony could be maintained by the two empires throughout the war. Austrian interests were ignored already in the Schlieffen Plan, and the Germans refused Austria's plea for assistance in putting an early end to Italy's involvement. It was almost impossible to concur in the treatment of Poland. Neither German nor Austro-Hungarian industrialists sanctioned the *Mitteleuropa* schemes of the German publicist Friedrich Naumann, who proposed a customs union stretching from Hamburg to Baghdad. Finally, the German military paid no heed to Austrian objections to the resumption of submarine warfare in 1917.

The basic reason for the absence of cooperation between the two powers was their inequality. National unrest, military setbacks, and industrial inadequacies all made Austria dependent on Germany. The Germans, understandably, soon developed an attitude of condescension, if not outright contempt, for their polyglot ally. The Austrians, naturally, were quick to take offense.

Emperor Karl and the Quest for Peace

Austro-German inequality was widened by the death of the venerable Franz Joseph on November 22, 1916, which deprived the Habsburg Monarchy of its most outstanding symbol of unity. Since signing the mobilization order in July 1914 the Emperor had become little more than a symbol, as the real business of state was taken over by the military. If only as a figurehead, however, he still would have been helpful in holding the Monarchy together during the last years of the war.

Franz Joseph had not been optimistic about the war's outcome even at the outset. When the archduchess Zita, the future Empress-Queen, congratulated him on an early victory, he replied:

> Yes, it is a victory, but that is the way my wars have always begun, only to finish in defeat. And this time it will be even worse. They will say I am old and cannot cope any more, and after that revolutions will break out and then it will be the end.[2]

The old Emperor's successor, Karl, the twenty-nine-year-old nephew of Franz Ferdinand, was poorly equipped for imperial leadership. His political education was not wholly neglected, as Franz Joseph had given him a personal tutorial every day the archduke was not at the front. But Karl had been heir to the throne for only two years, previously imagining that he would not be called to rule before the 1930s. There was simply too little time for him to learn all the intricacies of political life in the Dual Monarchy. He can be credited with a much more congenial personality than the dour Franz Ferdinand, and he made a genuine attempt to know his subjects at the per-

[2] Quoted in Gordon Brook-Shepherd, *The Last Habsburg* (New York: Weybright and Talley, 1968), p. 43.

Karl, Emperor-King of Austria-Hungary (1916–1918). *(New York Public Library)*

sonal level. He was particularly popular among common soldiers, with whom he would chat and share his meals.

In many ways Karl was the exact opposite of his great-
uncle, the late emperor. Simple and democratic, he greatly
reduced the elaborate court ceremonial, even holding audiences
in the open air. His informality extended to everyone, including
workers and peasants. Very much a man of the twentieth century, he relished the use of modern conveniences and had the
imperial train equipped with the latest technological devices.
His pleasures were few and simple, family and religion being by
far the most important. He loved music, but preferred folk tunes
to opera or symphonies. The bulk of his reading consisted of
history and travel books.

Karl was no intellectual, but was endowed with fundamen-
tally sound instincts. He firmly opposed Germany's resumption
of unrestricted submarine warfare, even though he was supported by none of his own military advisers. He also objected
to the Germans smuggling Lenin into Russia, arguing propheti-
cally that chaos caused by the Bolshevik leader in Russia might
easily spread into Central Europe. Most of all, he recognized
the Monarchy's desperate need for an early peace and the danger of permanent dependency should Germany win a decisive
victory. At the same time, however, he lacked the firm con-
victions and strong will of his uncle. On occasion he was obsti-
nate, at other times indecisive. He was too trusting and found it
hard to think ill of anyone, even those disloyal to him. In peace-
time he might have made a better than average constitutional
monarch; but his character and ability were not equal to the
gigantic task he faced. In fairness it should be added that even
a ruler of superhuman talent might not have done much better
in his place.

The death of Franz Joseph and Karl's accession to the
throne marked a turning point in the war for Austria-Hungary.
The first two years produced some encouraging results. Although there had been enormous casualties, there had also been
gratifying victories. The year 1915 had even witnessed a superficial kind of prosperity, with full employment and harvests
only slightly below normal. The Dual Monarchy was unique

among the belligerents in not incarcerating enemy belligerents or degrading their culture. While the British were smashing the shops of German butchers and forbidding the playing of Beethoven's music, the Austrians were commemorating the 300th anniversary of Shakespeare's death. Prisoners of war, who by early 1917 numbered over 1,100,000, were treated humanely despite food shortages and the presence of 1,500,000 refugees in the western provinces.

By the end of 1916 the effects of the British blockade were becoming serious, particularly with regard to food. Shortages were caused in part by the fighting in Galicia and Bucovina, but even more by the conscription of peasants and the mounting desire of Magyars, Czechs, and Poles to hoard what meager surpluses they had. Every nationality was convinced that it was making unilateral sacrifices for other nationalities, a conviction already held before the war but intensified during the conflict.

To the miseries of economic privation were added severe restrictions on civil liberties, especially in the Austrian half of the Monarchy. Unlike the material conditions, however, the denial of individual freedom was most complete near the beginning of the war and then improved in its later stages. Until the spring of 1917 Austria was ruled by a military dictatorship. The least militaristic of the great powers before the war, Austria suddenly became the most militarized. Until 1917 it was the only belligerent without an active parliament and with its government, administration, and economy thoroughly controlled by military officials.

For years it had been something of a truism within the Monarchy and abroad — among both civilians and the military — that should a major European war occur, Austria-Hungary would be engaged in a struggle for survival. It was taken for granted in both military and civilian circles that Austria's survival could be purchased only through extraordinary emergency measures. The Supreme Command of the Austro-Hungarian army had long been critical of the relaxed attitude of civilian officials toward disaffection among non-German Austrians. The war now presented military leaders with an opportunity to deal ruthlessly with all "traitors." By an unfortunate coincidence military powers were most dictatorial in war zones, which almost invariably were inhabited by nationalities already having an acute sense of oppression.

As in all belligerent states, the requirements of modern warfare necessitated a high degree of centralization. But the history of the Habsburg Monarchy had already demonstrated that centralization could not be distinguished from Germanization. This was especially true of the First World War when Austria was fighting side by side with the German Empire. The German Kaiser did not help matters by describing the war as a life-and-death struggle between Germans and Slavs. Germanization in Austria now became more than purely superficial. The German Austrians were undoubtedly the most consistent backers of the war, and bellicose Pan-German propaganda was on the rise. In January 1916 German was even made the official language of Bohemia. To the non-Germans of Austria these actions by military authorities were not something inevitable or transient, but a characteristic reversion to type.

The military dictatorship was gradually brought to an end by Karl's anxiety to appease public opinion both at home and abroad. The late winter and early spring of 1917 witnessed the relaxation of military discipline in factories and a general amnesty for Slavs convicted of political crimes, including high treason. At the end of May the Reichsrat resumed its deliberations. The reconvening of Parliament, in addition to the Emperor's widely recognized longing for peace, made a favorable impression in the West—so much so, in fact, that *emigré* Slav politicians working for the dismemberment of Austria were gravely worried. Within the Monarchy itself, however, German Austrians, Magyars, and especially members of the army, considered the amnesty a coddling of traitors. Far from placating the Austro-Slavs, it was seen by them as a sign of weakness. Even the resumption of Parliament was of mixed benefit to the state. Franz Joseph and his leading advisers had been apprehensive that such a move would lead to national conflicts damaging to Austria's reputation in the West. Developments during the last eighteen months of the Reichsrat existence proved Franz Joseph to have been a shrewd prognosticator.

From the reconvening of the Reichsrat until the early part of 1918 the political parties, on the whole, reaffirmed their loyalty to the state. Slav politicians insisted on the federalization of Austria or even of the whole Dual Monarchy, but few were at first outspokenly hostile to the existence of the state. Karl was careful not to take Austria's constitutional oath (although he was unable to resist Magyar pressure to take the Hungarian oath) in order to keep open the possibility of constitutional changes, but as before the war, most Germans and Magyars fervently opposed such reforms; even the Slavs could not agree on any comprehensive program.

Karl's liberalization of Austrian political life was in large measure due to his sincere desire to please his subjects and court the favor of the West. It also resulted from two international events of earth-shaking proportions in the early months of 1917: the overthrow of the Tsarist regime in Russia and the intervention of the United States. The complexion of the war changed almost immediately; now the democratic states were all in one camp, the monarchical-authoritarian states in the other. Forces favoring republicanism were given an immense boost.

The Russian Revolution made its greatest impact on the Social Democratic parties of Austria and Germany. They had supported the war primarily from the conviction that they were fighting the most reactionary and repressive government in Europe. The Revolution now made the war seem senseless.

American intervention meant that the prospects of an eventual Entente victory were decidedly improved; Austrian secessionists were encouraged, loyalists disheartened. But the sense of euphoria or depression was not constant after April 1917. Although the United States undoubtedly strengthened the Entente side, it did not immediately favor the destruction of Austria-Hungary. President Woodrow Wilson has become so closely identified with the principle of self-determination and the breakup of the Habsburg Monarchy that it is easy to forget that he adopted these policies only relatively late in the war. Both his critics and defenders have rightly described him as a moralist and idealist. Yet these characterizations tend to disguise his real aim in connection with Austria-Hungary, which until the late spring of 1918 was to induce it to sign a separate peace treaty, not to destroy it. He was first and foremost interested in the defeat of Imperial Germany; the Habsburg Monarchy was only a sideshow. As long as it appeared that the Reich could best be subdued by isolating it from its closest and most important ally, the President strove for a separate peace with Austria. When this course no longer seemed feasible, he reluctantly favored partitioning Germany's partner. In so doing he followed rather than led public opinion in the United States, albeit once the policy of self-determination was chosen he became its most eloquent and renowned spokesman.

The President's caution can be seen in his unwillingness to ask Congress for a declaration of war against Austria-Hungary until December 4, 1917, and then the move was made mainly to raise Italian morale. When he announced his famous "Fourteen Points" five weeks later, he was still anything but a radical nationalist advocating the rearrangement of the map of Europe along nationality lines. His Tenth Point did not go beyond mere autonomy for the Habsburg nationalities. Nothing was mentioned about possible independence for Czechoslovakia or Yugoslavia or the creation of a Greater Rumania. Austro-Hungarian authorities were more favorably disposed toward the speech than were advocates of total dismemberment of the Monarchy.

The attitude of the European Allies vis-à-vis the Dual Monarchy did not differ in any essential way from Wilson's. It is true that prior to intervention of the United States in the war they had committed themselves to slicing off various Habsburg provinces and territories; Tsarist Russia was to get Galicia; Italy was promised the Adriatic regions; Rumania was conceded southern Bucovina, Transylvania, and the Banat; and Serbia was to receive Bosnia-Herzegovina and southern Dalmatia. However, most of these territories had been acquired by the Habsburgs only since the eighteenth century and could not be considered part of the Monarchy's vital heartland. Most were economically and culturally backward; their loss would have actually increased Austro-Hungarian prosperity. Without them the Dual Monarchy would have been considerably less heterogeneous, and the prospects of political consolidation might have been enhanced. In their declaration of war aims in January 1917 the Entente did mention "national self-determination" for the smaller Habsburg nationalities. But the pronouncement was vague and not legally binding. The Italians wanted the Treaty of London fulfilled, but not a complete partition of Austria, which might create a rival South Slav state. The British Foreign Office favored the breakup of the Monarchy as early as 1916, but Prime Minister David Lloyd George, as well as countless influential individuals and organizations in the British Isles, were opposed to any radical territorial alterations in East Central Europe, especially if their pursuance might prolong the war or upset the balance of power. Numerous statements were issued by prominent Englishmen warning that the destruction of the Dual Monarchy would eventually redound to the benefit of Germany or Russia.

In the United States there was little interest in the Habsburg nationalities during the first several months of military involvement. The Department of State, including Secretary of State Robert Lansing, was anti-Habsburg. But a special group of experts gathered together by the President and known as the "Inquiry" was opposed to dissolution, principally on economic grounds. In France, feeling against the Monarchy was more pronounced than in either Britain or the United States; even so, the official French policy favored a separate peace. This policy was in fact shared by all the Western Powers until the spring of 1918.

To achieve a separate peace, the West was willing to offer large bribes, but to make no sacrifices. In secret negotiations in August 1917 the French offered Austria Poland (with its boundaries of 1772), Bavaria, and Prussian Silesia in exchange for surrender of the Italian Trentino and Trieste. No pressure was put on Italy by Paris to abandon the London Treaty, however, because of French fears that an indignant Italy might leave the alliance. In December of the same year the British proposed giving Austria-Hungary all of Poland, the South Slav areas not already in the Monarchy, and the Regat; the Habsburg

Monarchy for its part would federalize and sign a separate treaty. It was curious, to say the least, that the West regarded Austria-Hungary as a German tool, yet expected it to break with its partner.

These and several other private negotiations all proved unproductive for two simple reasons: Austria's unwillingness, and, more important, its inability to conclude a separate peace. The Austro-Slavs, and even some of the German Austrians and Magyars, would have been willing to desert the German alliance in the later stages of the war. Karl too may have occasionally entertained such thoughts. Realistically, however, such a move was completely out of the question until the very last days of the fighting. It is both militarily and psychologically dangerous to leave an alliance in the middle of a war, as was shown by Russia in 1917 and Italy in 1943. It was particularly hard for the Habsburg Monarchy because its army had been merged with Germany's since 1916 and was under the direction of German officers. The close proximity of Germany meant that a separate peace would immediately be accompanied by a German military occupation. A sudden foreign policy reversal, moreover, might have sparked a civil war in the Monarchy. Most German Austrians and Magyars continued to support the alliance as long as there was any chance of victory. The problem of a separate peace was therefore basically the same as that presented by federalization: Should the government exchange the allegiance of the powerful and loyal nationalities for the dubious favors of the smaller and weaker ones? That this was no imaginary dilemma was demonstrated when Karl did at last renounce the German compact on October 27, 1918. Almost at once Habsburg loyalism among the German Austrians and Magyars vanished into thin air.

The Allied Decision to Dismember Austria-Hungary

The failure to split the Austro-German alliance did not at first discourage the Allies. Anti-Habsburg sentiment was not commonplace in the West until far into 1918. To be sure, unfriendly feelings toward Austria had existed in some quarters since the beginning of the war and earlier. In Britain, liberal nationalists such as Steed and Seton-Watson at once became active proponents of the anti-Austrian movement. The latter founded a journal in October 1916 known as the *The New Europe* which was dedicated to a Europe rebuilt on nationality lines. Neither the contributors nor the readers were numerous, but they made up in influence what they lacked in numbers.

The Allied urge for an all-out military victory became apparent in the fall of 1917 when Vittorio Orlando and Georges Clemenceau became the premiers of Italy and France. The two men were advocates of an uncompromising peace and both eventually favored the political annihilation of Austria-Hungary. In the spring of 1918 Clemenceau and the Habsburg foreign minister, Count Ottokar Czernin, came to verbal blows after Czernin revealed that secret negotiations had taken place the previous year between Austria and France. Clemenceau was infuriated at the insinuation that the initiative had come from France and revealed that it had actually been the Austrian Emperor who had taken the lead in an attempt to gain a separate peace. The last charge was untrue, but Clemenceau was correct in adding that Karl had recognized the legitimacy of the French claim to Alsace-Lorraine. This so-called Sixtus Affair ended in the resignation of Czernin and a hurried trip by Karl to Germany to assure the Kaiser of his undying fidelity. Karl did not bind Austria-Hungary to any commitments, but the episode had the aspect of a "pilgrimage to Canossa." To the outside world the two countries now looked inseparable.

The Sixtus Affair coincided with the cessation of hostilities on the eastern front following the treaties of Brest Litovsk and Bucharest, which the Central Powers signed with Russia and Rumania in March and May 1918. With hundreds of thousands of German troops now available for service in the West and with the outcome of the war hanging in the balance, the Allies felt they needed to exploit every possible advantage if a military catastrophe were to be averted. Moreover, Bolshevik propaganda favoring complete national self-determination, loudly proclaimed at Brest Litovsk, could not go unanswered if the Bolsheviks were not to gain a permanent advantage in the battle for men's minds.

The most convenient way to compensate for the loss of Russia was the demolition of the Habsburg Monarchy. This could not be achieved by ordinary military measures because of Austria-Hungary's impregnable geographic defenses. And since a separate peace with Austria was no longer practical politics, Allied leaders thought that dismemberment was the only alternative. With some reluctance, this was the choice they made in the spring of 1918.

The ultimate solution of the Austrian problem was rationalized by the liberal nationalist argument that the causes of war could be removed if only the nationalities of East Central Europe were given governments and boundaries of their choice. The new states (presumably) having long traditions of anti-Germanism and, in some cases, occupying former German or German Austrian territories, would have a vested interest in joining the West against possible future German aggression. They would be "an insurmountable barrier" to German or Russian expansion into southeastern Europe.

Domestic politics in the West also played a role in the final decision to partition the Habsburg Monarchy. All four Allied leaders were sensitive to domestic charges that their foreign policy was either too harsh and therefore an impediment to a compromise peace of reconciliation, or too lenient, a course which would allow enemy powers to seek revenge in the near future. By breaking up the Monarchy both liberals and conservatives could be appeased. Liberals were delighted with the Allied determination to bring the blessings of self-determination and democracy to the "oppressed" nationalities of East Central Europe. Conservatives were won over by the idea of crushing Germany's most important ally. Probably no other policy toward the Central Powers could have received such widespread support.

"National self-determination" thus became the Allied goal. When President Wilson, on May 29, 1918, announced his intention to liberate the Habsburg nationalities, the war became more than ever a crusade, particularly in the English-speaking countries. This movement tended to blur the original reason for the new policy, namely military expediency; only to a much smaller extent was it based on moral or idealistic considerations. Many historians, dismayed at the results of the partition of Austria, have confused the issue by contending that the downfall of Austria-Hungary was "inevitable" with or without a change in Allied policy. This may or may not be true. But when the Allies made their decision to liquidate Austria-Hungary, they did not assume this to be a process that would take place automatically. It was assumed, however, that dissolution of the Habsburg Monarchy would be a positive good, since it would facilitate the establishment of a stable peace.

Despite this prevailing thought, many leaders in the West, including British Chief of Staff Sir Henry Wilson, U. S. Secretary of State Robert Lansing, and Premier Clemenceau of France, regarded their Austro-Hungarian policy as merely provisional and tactical, as late as October 1918. But for Woodrow Wilson and most of the American people, who had taken the "oppressed" Habsburg nationalities under their guardianship, there was no turning back once the new course had been set. In this sense, President Wilson's enormous prestige and oratorical talent, together with the pivotal military power of the United States, made Wilson's policy toward Austria more important than the views of all other Allied statesmen combined.

Psychological propaganda was one of the means used to encourage centrifugal forces in the Habsburg Monarchy. After the war many Germans, including Adolf Hitler, congratulated the Allies on the efficacy of their propaganda. The praise was perhaps misplaced. The Allies were neither the first to employ it nor necessarily the most successful in its use. From the outset of the war Germany utilized propaganda to help subvert the loyalty of Russian national minorities to the Tsarist government. The German example may have persuaded the Allies to use the same weapon against Germany's vulnerable ally, Austria. In any event, the Allies first began to direct propaganda against the Habsburg Monarchy on a large scale in the summer of 1918. Favorite techniques included dropping defeatist literature on

Austro-Hungarian trenches from airplanes, balloons, or rockets, and playing Slavic folk songs over phonographs. Leaflets accused the Habsburgs of racial discrimination, oppression, imperialism, and wartime atrocities. The impact of this propaganda is hard to evaluate, although it is improbable that it was decisive in the demise of the Monarchy.

More important than psychological warfare were undoubtedly the activities of *emigré* representatives of the smaller Habsburg nationalities. The Czechs, thanks to their armies in France, Italy, and especially Siberia, organized from Czech Austro-Hungarian prisoners of war, gained Allied recognition of their national council (located in Paris) not only as an ally, but also as a *de facto* government. Just the same, their importance as contributors in the destruction of Austria-Hungary can be exaggerated. The *emigrés* have either been praised by their countrymen as liberators, or denounced by pro-Habsburg writers as traitors who duped Allied leaders into dismembering a perfectly healthy state. Actually, the exiled politicians had very little to show for their efforts until the summer of 1918, even though they had begun their machinations soon after the war began. The Allies took them seriously only *after* deciding that Austria had to be destroyed.

The real significance of the exiles' movements lies less in the effect they had on the downfall of the Monarchy than in the general shape the postwar Successor States were to take. The *emigrés* were able to convince Allied statesmen long before the end of the war that Czechs and Slovaks were simply two branches of the same nationality and that Serbs, Croats, and Slovenes all longed to join a single state.

By far the most successful of the exiles were the two Czechs: Masaryk (a converted Slovak) and his former student Beneš. The pair shrewdly argued the case for Czechoslovak independence, not so much on the principle of self-determination as on the pragmatic usefulness of a Czech state to European stability. They also stressed the affinity of Czech democratic traditions to political values held in the West. Masaryk was skillful in clothing his *Realpolitik* in the mantle of lofty idealism so typical of the crusading spirit of 1918.

The South Slav exiles were much less effective than their Czech counterparts. No leader with the prestige and charisma of a Masaryk was at hand, and the Serbian government was uncooperative. The Yugoslav movement had originated entirely within the Habsburg Monarchy and was confined mainly to the Croats. Serbs, especially in the Kingdom of Serbia, were interested simply in Pan-Serbism. Insofar as they showed any interest in the Croats or Slovenes, the latter were regarded as people who might be annexed, or at best liberated, but they were not seen as potential partners in a future Greater Serbian state. These prejudices endured long after the war.

Following the intervention of Italy and the defeat of both Serbia and its benefactor, Russia, the Serbian government began to seek closer relations with the Habsburg exiles. Even then, the move did not stem from Yugoslav idealism but was made as a tactical device to please Entente partisans of a Yugoslav state. On July 20, 1917, the so-called Declaration of Corfu, signed between the "Yugoslav committee" representing the Austro-Hungarian *emigrés,* and the Serbian prime minister, Nikola P. Pašić, announced the intention of the Serbs, Croats, and Slovenes to form a united state on the basis of national and religious equality. Yugoslav unity now became the official policy of the Serbian government, and the Allies were presented with a united South Slav front. Nonetheless, the Allies did not formally recognize a Yugoslav state until after the war.

The Last Days of the Habsburg Monarchy

Probably more important than the activities of the exiles in precipitating the Monarchy's final collapse was the action of the Austro-Hungarian army. Its responsibility was strange: it did its duty too well. Despite tremendous setbacks (before the end of 1916 it had suffered the loss of 1.5 million prisoners and nearly twice that number missing, wounded, or killed out of a total of 7.5 million enrolled soldiers), it continued to wage war with considerable success, and troop morale remained high until the summer of 1918. At the battle of Caporetto in the autumn of 1917 Italy was nearly eliminated from the ranks of

the Allies. Total victory was denied only because of the insuffi-
ciency of Austrian and German transport and the flooding of
the Piave River. Vast booty and 275,000 prisoners were captured
in this, the most spectacular offensive by either side in three
years. Yet Caporetto created a paradox. The Italian people at
last began to take the war seriously and refused to capitulate.
German Austrians and Magyars, overjoyed by the battle,
abandoned thoughts of a compromise peace, demanding instead
a peace through victory. If the Austro-Hungarian army had not
fought so well, not only at Caporetto, but throughout most of the
war, the Allies might have triumphed much sooner. The Dual
Monarchy no doubt would have lost several peripheral provinces, but could have survived as a political unit.

Caporetto was the last great Habsburg victory. Another
offensive was foolishly undertaken in June of 1918, at Germany's
insistence, but it turned into a fiasco. The Italian army, re-
grouped and buttressed by English, French, and even some
American support, had attained numerical equality with the
exhausted, underfed, and poorly equipped Austrians. The
Habsburg offensive sputtered to a halt in ten days; no apprecia-
ble ground was conquered, and the Austro-Hungarians suffered 140,000 casualties. The army's fighting capacity was
practically finished. In the unlikely event that Karl had gathered
up enough courage and determination to crush secessionist
movements with the use of force, that force would have been
unavailable. The failure of the June offensive, along with
Germany's defeats in July and August, now convinced wavering
elements in the Monarchy that the war was irretrievably lost.

The disintegration of Habsburg loyalism was in many
respects a last-minute affair. Until the summer of 1917 those
Habsburg nationalities that had been reliable adherents of the
dynasty before the war remained faithful to the crown. This was
especially true of the Hungarian minorities among whom centrifugal movements were almost nonexistent. Slovaks and
Ruthenes who agitated for independence were nearly all emi-
grants living in the United States! On the other hand, increasing
restlessness was displayed by the Rumanians of Hungary, particularly after the intervention of the Regat in the autumn of 1916.

As always, the most dangerous national movement belonged to the Magyars, who persisted in their claim for a separate army, the annexation to Hungary of Austrian Dalmatia and Bosnia-Herzegovina, and the reduction of the Austrian tie to a purely personal union. What made these demands so pernicious was Austria's dependence on food from Hungary, an advantage the Magyars relentlessly exploited. With most of the Austro-Hungarian army engaged beyond the boundaries of the Monarchy and Austrian urbanites already suffering from malnutrition, the Magyars could prevent constitutional reform anywhere in the Monarchy simply by halting food shipments to Austria.

As might be expected, the non-German nationalities of Austria during the last two years of the war were much less complacent than the non-Magyars of Hungary. Whereas the latter generally asked for nothing more than national autonomy, the former made it clear, when the Reichsrat reconvened, that they would settle for nothing less than federalism. Until the beginning of 1918, however, out-and-out secession was not a part of their agenda, and the influence of emigrant politicians on those staying at home was still negligible. More often than not exile operations were denounced and repudiated.

It was only in the last ten months of the fighting that the lesser nationalities turned against the Monarchy. In the winter of 1917–1918 food and fuel shortages in the larger cities were appalling. All nationalities were disappointed by the slow progress of the peace talks at Brest Litovsk. Fearing that a settlement was being delayed by annexationist designs, the Austrian Social Democrats organized a massive general strike in January which spread to the Austro-Hungarian fleet in Pola. When the treaty with Russia was finally concluded in March, the Austrian Poles were incensed by the cession of a small section of Polish Russia (Cholm) to the newly independent state of the Ukraine. Neither the Treaty of Brest Litovsk nor that signed with Rumania at Bucharest came close to realizing the expectations for increased supplies of food. Instead of rations, Austria-Hungary received 2 million hungry prisoners of war, many of them infected by the antimonarchist and antiaristocratic Bolshevik ideology. Then in the summer months of 1918 came the series of Austro-German military disasters.

The *coup de grâce* for the Habsburg Monarchy was the collapse of the Bulgarian front on September 27. Common sense dictated that the Austro-Hungarian army could not hope to hold a second theater of war; Allied military occupation of the Monarchy was now only a matter of weeks, unless forestalled by an immediate armistice. On October 4 Vienna frantically begged Wilson for a cease-fire on the basis of the President's Fourteen Points. Since the Tenth Point had called for the federalization of the Dual Monarchy, Karl now made a hasty effort to comply. On October 16 he issued a manifesto asking Reichsrat deputies to form national councils as the foundation of a confederation of autonomous states linked only by a common allegiance to the Habsburg dynasty.

Karl was not simply being opportunistic in making this eleventh-hour move. He had been a convinced advocate of federalism and national equality long before mounting the throne. The tragedy was that federalization of the Monarchy was not even thinkable until the late summer of 1918 when most German Austrians and Magyars were finally convinced of the inevitability of defeat. Yet by then the "submerged" nationalities were in no mood to consider anything short of outright independence. Only a reform imposed by the West would have stood any chance of success at this late date. But this would have necessitated an Allied occupation of the Monarchy. Military occupation was used for similar purposes in Germany and Japan after World War II, and with great success. Karl and his last Austrian prime minister, Professor Heinrich Lammasch, would have welcomed such an occupation. The idea was opposed, however, by President Wilson, who rejected, as a matter of principle, the use of American troops for the enforcement of political reforms. In any event, it would have been incomprehensible to Allied public opinion if their leaders had suddenly reversed the policy of complete national independence for the Monarchy's nationalities. This was especially true in the United States, where politicians were busy cultivating the favors of East Central European voters for Congressional elections.

Whatever slight possibility there might have been for the success of a last-minute reform was ruined by the stipulation in Karl's manifesto limiting federalization to the Austrian half of the Monarchy. The restriction meant that the Czechs and Slovaks, Rumanians, Ruthenes, and South Slavs would be politically separated, with some of them remaining under Magyar domination.

Even though Karl, in issuing the manifesto, took care not to violate his oath to the Hungarian constitution in which he had pledged to defend the kingdom's territorial integrity, the Hungarian Diet used the attempted federalization of Austria as a pretext for renouncing the *Ausgleich* and seceding from the Dual Monarchy. With the old order crumbling on every side, the Magyar ruling class clung to its delusion that Hungary's integrity could be maintained by the mere act of separation from Austria. Instead, the secession of Hungary only set a precedent for nationally conscious members of its own minorities.

Karl's manifesto won the favor of neither the Habsburg nationalities nor President Wilson. On October 19 Wilson replied to the Austro-Hungarian note of October 4 by stating that his recent recognition of a *de facto* Czechoslovak government had invalidated his Tenth Point; the Czechoslovaks and also the Yugoslavs now had to be the judges of their own destinies.

Many writers, including some sympathetic to the Habsburg cause, have contended that Wilson was doing nothing more than recognizing accomplished facts. This is simply not true. No Czechoslovak government existed in Prague on October 19, let alone one that exercised *de facto* authority. And there was as yet no indication that the Slovaks intended to break away from Budapest. A Yugoslav state joining together Serbs, Croats, and Slovenes was not organized until December 1, 1918. Wilson was anticipating and helping to create accomplished facts, not sanctioning them.

But the Austro-Hungarian Foreign Ministry was in no position to argue. In its reply of October 27, it recognized the right of North and South Slavs to full independence and made a new request for a cease-fire. Only now did the Slavs actually secede from Viennese rule—actions which the central government made no attempt to resist. Similarly, the German-Austrian Provisional National Assembly (organized on October 21), offended by the dynasty's last-minute bid for a separate peace, assumed full legislative powers on the 30th. Two weeks later, it declared German-Austria a republic.

In the last days of October and the early part of November the only remnants of the ancient Habsburg Monarchy were the Emperor-King, a shadow cabinet, and the Austro-Hungarian army. The army's condition had deteriorated badly since its abortive June offensive. Food supplies were so low that many soldiers in base camps "deserted" to the battle lines where rations were slightly better. Along one section of the Italian front the average weight of the soldiers was a pathetic 120 pounds. Uniforms were in rags; weapons, munitions, and horses were hopelessly inadequate. The national revolutions of late October had cut off fresh supplies. Requests for an armistice, along with Karl's manifesto, had made continued bloodshed senseless. Creation of national states encouraged whole regiments to return to their homes. Nevertheless, when the Allies launched a final offensive on the 24th of October, the vestiges of the Austro-Hungarian army resisted heroically for several days. On the 27th, however, the lines began to melt away and on the 31st the army command agreed to an armistice. Austrian troops ceased firing on November 3, but owing to a misunderstanding the Italians continued hostilities for another thirty-six hours. In the interval 300,000 unresisting Austro-Hungarian soldiers were captured. As late as 1964 an Italian historian would describe this as "the glorious Battle of Vittorio Veneto, in which the Austrians were eliminated from the war."[3] Italy's honor was redeemed and Italy could enter the Peace Conference expecting to harvest the fruits of its "victory."

On November 11, 1918, Emperor Karl "renounced any participation in the business of the [Austrian] State."[4] Two days

[3] Piero Pieri, "The Italian Front," in Vincent J. Esposito (ed.), *A Concise History of World War I* (New York: Praeger, 1964), p. 161.
[4] Quoted in C. A. Macartney, *The Habsburg Empire, 1790–1918* (New York: Macmillan, 1969), p. 833.

later he issued a similar proclamation for Hungary. The 640-year rule of the Habsburg dynasty was at an end.

The Monarchy's Fall: Who Was Responsible?

The "fall" of any empire is always the product of numerous events, forces, and personalities whose exact causal significance can never be measured with anything like scientific precision. In the case of Austria-Hungary, the First World War was the decisive catalyst. Habsburg statesmen, hoping for *"einen kleinen Herbstspaziergang"* (a short autumn stroll) through Serbia soon found themselves entangled in a prolonged conflict from which extrication was impossible. Austria-Hungary's internal structure, suitable for economic and cultural vigor in times of peace, was too fragile to withstand the demands of modern warfare. The Monarchy might have endured one, two, or even three years of fighting; the fourth year was too much.

Austria-Hungary, along with Serbia and Russia, most scholars agree, was one of the states most guilty of instigating the war. On the other hand, once the war had begun, the Dual Monarchy made greater efforts than any other country to bring it to an early end. That the war dragged on for over four years was the fault of Germany, France, and Italy, probably in that order. After incredible losses in blood and treasure those states dared not make peace without substantial territorial compensation if domestic revolutions were to be averted. In that sense, Germany in particular bears a major share of the blame for the downfall of the Habsburg Monarchy.

It is true that the Allies contributed to the protraction of the war; they also deliberately set out to destroy the Monarchy in May 1918. All the same, their efforts would have been fruitless if the Monarchy's long-term internal problems, intensified by the war, had not made it already ripe for elimination. Allied determination to destroy the Monarchy, moreover, never approached fanaticism. It is hard to imagine that the Allies would have prevented the Habsburgs from saving their state if the latter could have done so on their own.

Allied responsibility can be discovered less in the fall of

the Monarchy than in the shape which the New Europe was to take. The Habsburgs had consistently discouraged nationalism in East Central Europe. The Allies intentionally encouraged it, naively expecting it to promote the cause of international cooperation. Like the classical laissez-faire economists they saw a natural harmony of interests between independent nations. They now fostered the birth of new states which they later had neither the ability nor the desire to defend. They were the midwife to movements that twenty years later would nearly devour them.

CHAPTER THREE

The
Patchwork
Treaties

Before the Conference

The Treaty of Versailles with Germany has aroused passionate controversy for more than half a century. Yet curiously enough, few historians have shown much interest in the so-called lesser treaties of St. Germain and Trianon. These two treaties nonetheless established not only the boundaries of Austria and Hungary, but most of the frontiers of the new or greatly enlarged states of East Central Europe as well. In large measure the treaties also set the pattern of domestic affairs and international relations of the Successor States during the interwar period.[1]

[1] Scholars interested in the documentation for certain aspects of this chapter should see the author's article entitled, "The Patchwork Treaties: St. Germain and Trianon Reconsidered," published in *The Rocky Mountain Social Science Journal,* vol. IX, No. 2 (April, 1972).

The standard interpretation of St. Germain and Trianon, still found in many textbooks on modern European history, contends that the treaties, if perhaps imperfect in details, were the best possible under the circumstances existing in 1919. Here and there small minorities may have been left under alien rule, but the confused ethnographic map of East Central Europe made this inevitable. Certainly no earlier peace settlement had granted self-determination to so many. If mistakes were made they resulted from *faits accomplis* carried out by the Secessionist States—Czechoslovakia, Poland, Rumania, and Yugoslavia—that had militarily occupied coveted territory before the Peace Conference even met. The Big Four Powers—France, Britain, the United States, and Italy—weary of war and rapidly demobilizing lacked the physical power to compel the new states to withdraw from the contested territories. Their only remaining task, therefore, was to arbitrate minor disputes.

The orthodox interpretation, of course, is by no means pure nonsense. Obviously the existence of ethnic "islands," for example, did make it impossible to draw boundaries that would not create national minorities. It is equally clear that hatred between the Successor States would have made any peace settlement, no matter how equitable, unsatisfactory in the eyes of chauvinists. To argue, however, that the Allies were innocent bystanders, helpless to prevent the *faits accomplis,* or that they were impartial arbiters at Paris, is simply to fly in the face of the facts.

As early as June 29, 1918, France had pledged its support to Czech claims for the historic borders of the Bohemian crownlands. Two months later the British Foreign Office recognized the future union of Czechs and Slovaks under a single government. The significance of President Wilson's recognition of a Czechoslovak government in early September, and the aspirations of the Yugoslavs for independence in October, have already been mentioned. In the Austro-Italian armistice of November 3, the Allied Supreme War Council gave the Italians permission to occupy Austro-Hungarian territory up to the line promised them in the Treaty of London. Four days later a separate armistice with Hungary was concluded at Belgrade by the

French commander of a Franco-Serbian army, General Franchet d'Esperey, who demanded that Hungarian troops evacuate southern and eastern Hungary. In a matter of days, Serbian and Rumanian soldiers took over territories claimed by their governments.

The Belgrade truce made no mention of northern Hungary, but on December 3 Edvard Beneš, now the Czech foreign minister, gained French sanction for the Czech army to occupy and administer Slovakia. On the 19th, Paris informed the Ballhausplatz in Vienna of a similar Czech right in the disputed German districts of the Historic Provinces even though this action violated the Austro-Italian armistice of November 3. The armistice had stipulated that Habsburg territory would be considered as a unit and would not be divided prior to the Peace Conference.

In the summer of 1919, when the Czech army was being driven out of Slovakia by the Hungarian Bolsheviks, the Supreme War Council in Paris insisted that the German Austrians supply the Czechs with war material. France had in the meantime established a "very strong Military Mission" in Prague "and her officers [were] in command of the Czecho-Slovak army."[2] In the considered opinion of the British representative in Prague "had it not been for the skill and energy displayed by the French generals in the field and their staff, the whole of Slovakia must have fallen into the hands of the Magyars."[3] The conclusion is inescapable that from the summer of 1918 to the summer of 1919 the Allies were anticipating, helping to create, and sanctioning the *faits accomplis* of the Secessionist States.

The argument that once the *faits accomplis* had taken place the Allies were powerless to change them is without much substance. The Allies cajoled the Czechs, Serbs, and Rumanians into evacuating Hungarian territory, although in the case of the Rumanians the withdrawal came only after months of looting

---

[2] E. L. Woodward and Rohan Butler (eds.), *Documents on British Foreign Policy, 1919–1939,* First Series, vol. VI, *Mr. Gosling (Prague) to Earl Curzon (received, January 14, 1920),* Prague, December 31, 1919, p. 544. Hereafter referred to as *DBFP,* 1st.

[3] *Ibid., Mr. Gosling (Prague) to Earl Curzon (received July 14, 1919),* p. 71.

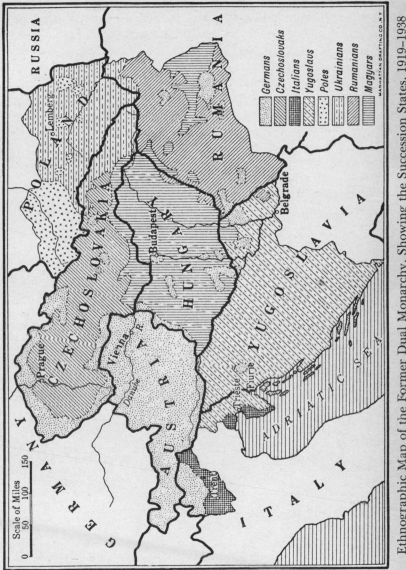

Ethnographic Map of the Former Dual Monarchy. Showing the Succession States, 1919-1938

and after innumerable threats and pleas by the Big Four. Only in White Russian and Ukrainian territories conquered by the Poles were the Allies unable to exercise their authority.

The unvarnished fact is that the territorial terms of the treaties of St. Germain and Trianon conformed nearly everywhere to the exact wishes of the Big Four. If the *faits accomplis* made any difference at all, it was only in the later stages of the Conference when the Allies began to have doubts about the wisdom of some of their decisions.

The Territorial Commissions and the American Representatives

The Big Four—Wilson, Clemenceau, Lloyd George, and Orlando—imposed their will on all the Successor States, but in a manner highly prejudicial to Austria and Hungary. The delegations of the Secessionist States had ample opportunity to present their case orally to the Allies. Since Austria and Hungary were not represented at the Conference until the later stages, their counterarguments had to be supplied by the Allies themselves.

The Big Four theoretically had the last word in all territorial decisions, but in practice most boundary disputes were decided by territorial commissions composed of technical experts from each of the Allied states. The arrangement was probably a good one in principle, since the Western leaders had little knowledge of East Central Europe. The use of expert advisers and scientists, it was widely believed, would mark a radical departure in the very nature of peacemaking. Henceforth boundaries would presumably be based not on chance, force, fear, greed, or compromise, but on exact knowledge. No longer would self-seeking diplomats and politicians be making the decisions, but dispassionate scientists.

The reality proved to be far different from the ideal. The "experts" were not always knowledgeable on the particular problems they were asked to solve; their objectivity was likewise not beyond reproach. Harold Nicolson, himself one of the British commissioners, confessed that we thought less about our late enemies than about the new countries which had arisen from their tired loins. . . . It was the thought of the new Serbia, the new Greece, the new Bohemia, and the new Poland which made our hearts sing at heaven's gate. . . . Bias there was, and prejudice. But they proceeded not from any revengeful desire to subjugate and penalize our late enemies, but from a fervent aspiration to create and fortify the new nations which we regarded with maternal instinct, as the justification of our sufferings and our victory.[4]

Equally unfortunate was the failure of the Big Four to give specific instructions to the various commissions. They were simply admonished to disregard political considerations and to consider economic unity and defense as well as purely ethnographic factors. Most damaging of all was the absence of any central committee, other than the Big Four itself, with power to coordinate and oversee the findings of each commission. Separate commissions were organized for each of the Secessionist States in order to evaluate their claims, but each commission was allowed to work on only one state. When the decisions of all the commissions were combined in the treaties, it was discovered that Austria and Hungary had been dealt with far more harshly than intended. But now the territorial awards were irreversible.

Of all the commissioners, those from the United States were probably the best informed and the most impartial. The United States had no desire for territory or allies, being concerned solely with creating the conditions for a stable and lasting peace. If the Americans had a tendency to lean toward the new states, they were nevertheless more interested than other commissioners in reducing the size of ethnic minorities to a minimum. Unfortunately, the American experts had relatively little influence either on the commissions themselves (which were all headed by Frenchmen) or even on President Wilson. They frequently found themselves in a minority and were handicapped by their inexperience in negotiating. They were given no instructions by the President and were not even informed of his promises to other statesmen. When the President returned to the United States following the signing of the Treaty of Ver-

[4] *Peacemaking 1919* (New York: Grosset & Dunlap, 1965), pp. 32, 33.

sailles, American influence declined and was later destroyed by the Senate's refusal to ratify the Versailles Treaty.

Woodrow Wilson and the South Tyrol

The role of President Wilson in shaping the Peace Settlement in East Central Europe was less than is usually imagined. There is no doubt that he enjoyed enormous popularity and influence in both the secessionist and the defeated states: to the first group he was a liberator, to the second an impartial and all-powerful judge. Nonetheless, he largely ignored the region after the breakup of the Monarchy. The "Four Principles," which he had announced on February 11, 1918, did relate to the area in a general way. According to these principles each part of the Settlement was to be just; peoples and provinces were not to be shifted about without regard to their wishes or as a result of compromise between rival claimants. Finally, all "well defined national elements" were to be granted self-determination so long as new international problems were not created.

Nicolson directed a blistering attack against the President fourteen years after the Conference for not imposing these principles on friend and foe alike. The criticism is not entirely fair, as Wilson did not possess the unlimited power imagined by the British diplomat. He had to bargain and compromise (despite his Four Principles), as did all other delegates. Moreover, his physical and mental powers were impaired by a slight stroke on April 3, 1919, just at a time when the Big Four turned its attention to East Central European questions. But even if he had been in perfect health he could not have realized his principles entirely, since in the real world of international politics this was an impossibility. An adversary such as Clemenceau, popularly known as "The Tiger," could not simply be ignored or pushed aside. The President can be criticized not so much for betraying his own principles as for raising unrealistic hopes and expectations.

On one point, Nicolson's critique was fully justified: Wilson's support of Italian claims to the German-speaking South Tyrol. The area involved was petty by American standards, consisting of less than 3000 square miles and 225,000 people. But in making the offer Wilson broke every one of his Four Principles and the Ninth of his Fourteen Points which read: "A readjustment of the frontiers of Italy should be effected along clearly recognizable lines of nationality."[5] At the southern limit of the South Tyrol lay one of the clearest lines of nationality in Europe. Only 3 percent of the population of the South Tyrol was Italian, and the German population in the Trentino to the south amounted to only 14,000 of 390,000 souls.

The Italians argued that possession of the Brenner Pass was a strategic necessity. But even nineteenth-century Italian military experts were convinced that the Salurn gap between the South Tyrol and the Italian-speaking Trentino was as defensible as the Brenner. It had been Italy or Italian states, moreover, not Austria, which had initiated the wars with Austria between 1848 and 1915. To contend that Italy with its 38,000,000 people needed a strategic border against a nation of 6,500,000 was absurd. Even if a union had occurred between Austria and Germany, the German-speaking people would have been more a danger than a source of security for Italy. Austria countered the Italian argument of military necessity by offering to neutralize all of the Tyrol or to permit Italy to garrison the south. There is no evidence that either offer was considered by the Conference.

Unlike border disputes in other parts of East Central Europe, Wilson's responsibility in the South Tyrol question was unique. The British and French could not openly violate their commitments in the secret Treaty of London. The United States had not been a party to that agreement, although Wilson failed to denounce it. The American President was nevertheless the only man who could have given the South Tyroleans the kind of justice he had outlined in his Four Principles. Informed that his promise to Orlando violated these principles, Wilson pleaded "insufficient study." Yet we know that his adviser, Colonel Edward M. House, told the President about the German South Tyrol as early as October 1918.

One of the wisest of the American experts in Europe, Professor Archibald C. Coolidge, summed up the South Tyrol

[5] The *Congressional Record*, 65 Congress, 2d Session, pp. 680–681.

President Wilson with Mrs. Wilson at the Longchamps race course while in Paris for the Peace Conference. *(New York Public Library)*

controversy in a letter to the American Commission to Negotiate Peace (which included President Wilson).

> In no question of boundary at present under discussion have we more clearly the principles of history, nationality and self-determination on the one side and strategic and imperialistic considerations on the other. The case might be regarded as a test one under the Fourteen Points.[6]

The Sudeten Question

Self-determination was also clearly violated in western Czechoslovakia. The Czechs claimed the entire area—Bohemia, Moravia, and the old Austrian Silesia—because of its alleged historic, geographic, and economic unity, even though a third of the provinces' population (3,250,000) was German speaking.

The Czech arguments, while not without merit, were open to serious refutation. Historically, the Egerland in western Bohemia, with its one million Sudeten Germans, had had only the loosest association with Bohemia until the second half of the nineteenth century. Economically, the provinces were not as interdependent as Beneš maintained. The Czech foreign minister claimed that nearly all the industries of the Historic Provinces were in German districts. In reality, only 45.5 percent of the Sudetens were engaged in industry and mining compared to 39.4 percent of the Czechs, and Czechs owned an equally high percentage of industrial enterprises. Sudeten industries, moreover, tended to be of the luxury variety, hardly indispensable to the existence of the Czechoslovak state.

Even the related arguments of geographic unity and strategic necessity, long considered irrefutable by diplomats and historians alike, are lacking in logic. All of Austrian Silesia, a large part of northern Moravia, and three salients in northern Bohemia lay outside the interior watersheds. Northwestern

---

[6] *Papers Relating to the Foreign Relations of the United States, Paris Peace Conference, 1919*, vol. XII, No. 192, Vienna, April 7, 1919, p. 283. Hereafter referred to as *FRUS, PPC*.

Bohemia was exposed to Germany in the Elbe Valley, and only a low range of hills separated southern Bohemia and Moravia from Austria. Even where mountain ranges coincided with the boundaries of the Historic Provinces, they were not necessarily the only natural barriers to attack. In most sections there was a second range of mountains only slightly lower than those at the border. If the secondary range of mountains had been used as the political boundary, only about 700,000 Sudeten Germans would have remained in Czechoslovakia, while 163,000 Czechs would have been left outside the new state; the German-speaking population would have been reduced by 80 percent and the Czech borders would have been in areas with a friendlier population.

The Czech case for the Sudetenland was strengthened by the lack of any apparent alternative. Germany did not claim the Sudetenland, as a territorial increment in that region could only come at the expense of German territory elsewhere. The Austrian delegation wanted the area on the basis of self-determination, but offered no ideas on how the German-speaking areas in the north could possibly remain a part of the Austrian state when completely cut off by Czech territory. The Austrian solution made sense only if a union *(Anschluss)* took place between all German Austrian regions and Germany, a plan forbidden by the Allies. Even the Sudeten Germans themselves were lukewarm about joining Austria once the Austro-German union became impossible.

The Allies, especially the American experts and Lloyd George, were uneasy about the enormous German minority. The United States even proposed the cession of some border areas to Germany. Allied fears were quieted, however, by Beneš's assurance that Czechoslovakia would be made into "another Switzerland." The analogy was ill-chosen, since Czechoslovakia developed into a unitary nation-state. Indignant Sudeten Germans later used Beneš's promise as proof of Czech insincerity.

The Big Four decided to leave the historic borders of the Bohemian crownlands virtually intact, a victory for the French.

Their decision was understandable. For Germany to emerge from the war with a larger German-speaking population and more industries than it had had in 1914 would have been intolerable.

The Eastern Boundaries of Czechoslovakia

The French desire to see Czechoslovakia fortified territorially was also apparent in their support of Czech claims in the east. In these areas, belonging to Hungary for over a thousand years, the Czech case was based on principles diametrically opposed to those used in the Historic Provinces. Except for a halfhearted reference to the ninth-century "Greater Moravia," the historic argument was jettisoned in favor of ethnology. Since the Czech and Slovak languages were related, the Czech maintained that the two peoples were simply two branches of the same nationality artificially separated by historical events. As we observed earlier, the Allies had accepted this argument well before the end of the war, and it went unchallenged at the Conference. The rapid Czech military occupation of Slovakia in the waning days of 1918 and the beginning of 1919 was designed to prevent Slovak expressions of anti-Czech opinion which might contradict the theory of Czechoslovak solidarity. Prague allowed the Slovaks no representation at the Conference, and when their leader, Father Andrej Hlinka, attempted to protest the Czech-Slovak union, he was denied a passport and later arrested by the Czech government.

The Czech claim to Slovakia was reinforced by the so-called Pittsburgh Pact concluded in the Pennsylvania metropolis between Masaryk and American Slovak representatives on June 30, 1918. The agreement, which was endorsed and then repudiated by Father Hlinka, proclaimed Czech-Slovak unity in exchange for Slovak autonomy and representation at the Peace Conference. The Czechs later excused their failure to fulfill the autonomy pledge on the grounds that no understanding with American citizens could be legally binding. This was technically true, but ethically dubious. The Czechs were not troubled by legal scruples when using the Pact at the Conference as proof of Czechoslovak unity.

The only Slovak question considered by the Conference was the border with Hungary. Here Magyars and Slovaks lived side by side in a bewildering ethnic mosaic. Insofar as any ethnic line could be established it followed the southern edge of the Carpathian foothills. Lateral communications through southern Slovakia therefore seemed to require that a broad strip of the Hungarian plain be given to Czechoslovakia. Likewise, if the new state was to have a port on the Danube, the most convenient choice was Pressburg (Bratislava), the former capital of Hungary.

Despite American and Italian efforts to make the political boundary coincide as closely as possible with the ethnic line, the compromise reached by the Czechoslovak Territorial Commission still left about 855,000 Magyars in Slovakia compared to only 140,000 Slovaks in Hungary. But at least the extreme Czech claim, which would have placed 1,300,000 Magyars under Czechoslovak rule, was substantially reduced.

The eastern territories of Czechoslovakia were rounded out by the addition of Ruthenia. Inhabited by a majority of Ruthenes and a sizable Magyar Minority, the region contained neither Slovaks nor Czechs. Masaryk and Beneš had assumed during the war that the area would go to Russia, but the Revolution and the creation of a large Poland made that solution impossible. The existence of an overtly hostile Hungary to the south now made Czechoslovak leaders anxious to establish a direct territorial link with Rumania, a country with equal reason to fear Hungarian revenge. The Allies favored the Czech claim after Beneš promised to grant Ruthenia a special autonomous status and a separate diet. Ruthenia and eastern Slovakia (which had only a minority of Slovaks) added 160 miles to Czechoslovakia, making the country four times as long as it was wide and increasing the number of minorities by three-quarters of a million people. Coolidge thought that "the desire of the Czecho-Slovaks to obtain the Hungarian Ruthenian territory [was] based not so much on racial relationship as on imperialism, and [questioned] whether in the long run its satisfaction would not add to the dangers to which the new Czecho-Slovak state [was] exposed."[7]

The smallest of Czechoslovakia's territorial claims was also one of the most important for the country's future international relations: the duchy of Teschen. Its rich coal fields, heavy industry, and railroads connecting the Historic Provinces with Slovakia made the area especially attractive to the Czechs. But the population was a mixture of Czechs, Germans, and Poles, with the Poles having a majority. After the fall of the Habsburg Monarchy, the area was jointly occupied by Czech and Polish troops. When the Poles held parliamentary elections in their zone, Prague responded with a military occupation of the Polish district (January 23, 1919). The Czech premier, Karel Kramář, expected the Allies to sanction this move just as they had earlier Czech *faits accomplis*. This time he was mistaken. The French were disgusted, and the Poles, busy fighting the Russians in the east, were infuriated by this "stab in the back." Masaryk's hopes for strong Czech-Polish ties lay in ruins. The Allies tried to settle the issue by awarding the larger part of the area to Czechoslovakia; but the Poles, with 90,000 of their nationals living under Czechoslovak sovereignty, still seethed. For nineteen years the two Slavic states were to feud over the area.

Czechoslovakia's Assets and Debits

Superficially, Czechoslovakia emerged from the Peace Conference as the most generously endowed of the Successor States. All but its most extreme territorial demands had been met. With 13,374,000 people and 52,000 square miles, it ranked far ahead of both Austria and Hungary. If smaller than Poland, Rumania, or Yugoslavia, it was far more industrialized. It had retained its strategic defenses in Bohemia and enjoyed the almost unqualified support of France.

A closer look at the new state, however, revealed some unsettling facts. Less than two-thirds of the population (65.5

---

[7] *FRUS, PPC.* vol. XII, *Professor A. C. Coolidge to the Commission to Negotiate Peace,* No. 210, Vienna, April 11, 1919, p. 435.

percent) was Czechoslovak, and scarcely one-half was Czech. The Slovaks, although officially counted as a *Staatsvolk,* were often unenthusiastic about if not downright antagonistic to the union. Worse, Czechoslovakia was diplomatically isolated and landlocked. Of its 2550 miles of frontiers, only the 125 next to Rumania bordered on a friendly state. The French, and to a lesser extent the British, were nevertheless relying on 7 million Czechs to be an eastern bastion against 62 million Germans.

Austria at the Peace Conference

By the time the Austrian delegation was permitted to state its case before the Conference in June 1919, the meeting was four and a half months old. The South Tyrol had been assigned to Italy, and the Historic Provinces in their entirety had been given to Czechoslovakia.

The Austrians were housed, or it would be more accurate to say, imprisoned, in the chateau of St. Germain outside Paris. Like other enemy peace delegations, they were literally locked up, and their correspondence with the outside world was censored. At Clemenceau's insistence, they were allowed only two meetings with the Allies; beyond this their arguments had to be made in writing. The Paris Peace Conference was the first in modern European history where oral negotiations were prohibited.

Despite the humiliating arrangements, the Austrians received a friendlier reception in Paris than had been granted the Germans. The humble tone of the opening speech by the Austrian Chancellor, Karl Renner, was favorably contrasted in the Parisian press with the belligerent attitude taken by the head of the German delegation. The Austrians actually had no choice. They, unlike a good many Germans, were fully aware of their exhaustion by the war. Their neighbors, moreover, had occupied nearly all contested areas and were in a position to shut off vitally needed food supplies. Lacking military force and bargaining power, the Austrians wisely chose to rely on the ethnographic principle and the Wilsonian concept of a just peace in asking for only those territories of the old Monarchy inhabited by German majorities.

We have already seen how the Austrian program was realistic only if the German-speaking sections of the old Monarchy were joined to the new democratic German Republic. This was precisely Austria's intention as early as November 12, 1918, when the German-Austrian National Assembly appealed to Wilson and his principle of self-determination to allow the *Anschluss* with Germany. The larger part of the Austrian public supported this move with mixed emotions. The rough treatment meted out to the Habsburgs and the indifference shown toward the Austro-Hungarian army by Berlin during the war had been neither forgotten nor forgiven. Even the memory of the humiliation of 1866 was by no means dead. The Austrian Social Democrats were eager enough to join forces with their comrades in the Reich, but they and the Austrian Pan-Germans had no wish to see Austria obliterated altogether. A restoration of the loose relationship between Austria and other German states preceding the 1866 war would have satisfied most Austrians. A few, however, including monarchists and industrialists, were flatly opposed even to this arrangement.

The *Anschluss* movement attained real momentum only on the southern side of the Austro-German border. The German government and people no doubt would have been only too happy to see the annexation of their Alpine cousins, but realized, as in the Sudeten case, that any false move on Austria's account would damage their other claims. The British and Americans did not initially object to the proposed merger; Secretary of State Robert Lansing felt that to prevent such a union "was a dream." Once more, however, Anglo-American willingness to see self-determination fulfilled in East Central Europe was blocked by the French. The clash produced a pseudocompromise in which Austria was simply forced to agree not to "alienate its independence" without the unanimous approval of the Council of the League of Nations, an action which France alone could prevent. No one, least of all the Austrians, was fooled by this sophistry.

Austria's imposed independence was unprecedented in European history. Now that the fruit had officially been forbidden, the Austrians were more than ever convinced that *Anschluss* was precisely what they wanted. The small state was regarded as a prison, a punishment for losing the war. The only escape was an *Anschluss.*

When the Allies rejected the union with Germany the Austrian peace delegation concentrated on retaining German-speaking districts just beyond the provisional boundaries. One such area was the southern borderlands of Bohemia and Moravia where the census of 1910 had tallied a German-speaking population of 357,000 and only 18,500 Czechs. These predominantly agricultural lands sold their products to Linz and Vienna, where they were badly needed after the loss of Galicia and Hungary. Diminutive in size and population, the region nevertheless provided the Allies with an opportunity to demonstrate good-will to the demoralized Austrians. Lansing and the American experts supported the Austrian request. But President Wilson and the leaders of other Allied delegations favored the historic boundary. So only minor revisions were made in the Austro-Czech boundary, and those were beneficial to Czechoslovakia.

Austria's claims were given a more sympathetic hearing in the case of German West Hungary, or as it was soon called, the Burgenland. The preliminary draft of the treaty made no mention of the area. The Czechs had earlier requested a "corridor" to friendly Yugoslavia, but strong Italian opposition caused its rejection by the Big Four. Instead, Conference leaders agreed to transfer the region with its 285,000 people (80 percent of them German-speaking) to Austria, possibly as compensation for the loss of South Tyrol. Although the Hungarians resented this transfer, it did not stand in the way of friendly Austro-Hungarian relations during most of the interwar period.

A reasonably satisfactory border for Austria was also drawn with the new state of Yugoslavia. The Yugoslavs laid claim to all the major cities near the ethnic border, holding the Austrian census figures to be distorted. German speech in Carinthia and Styria was merely the product of a "Germanizing system of violence." The Yugoslav argument, which closely resembled that employed by Germany when claiming Alsace-Lorraine in 1871, was rejected by the Allies, and the disputed towns were divided: Radkersburg and Villach went to Austria and Marburg to Yugoslavia. In southern Carinthia a plebiscite favored Austria when 40 percent of the Slovenes in the district rejected incorporation into Yugoslavia. A similar plebiscite in the Marburg area almost certainly would have produced the same result. The loss of that town, the second largest in Styria, ruined Austria's best east-west communications. In all, over 65,000 German Styrians were assigned to Yugoslavia compared to 4000 Slovenes left in Austrian Styria. Still, Yugoslavia was the only Secessionist State denied a significant part of its claims against Austria.

When all the boundaries were finally settled the new Austria had a little over 32,000 square miles and 6.5 million people (1923) representing 26.5 percent of the population and 23 percent of the territory of the Austrian half of the Dual Monarchy. No less than a third of all the German-speaking people of old Austria were left under foreign rule, including roughly 650,000 just beyond the new frontiers. The country was now 96 percent German, the other 4 percent mainly Viennese Czechs and Carinthian Slovenes.

The nonterritorial aspects of the Treaty of St. Germain were fairly moderate when compared to similar clauses in the Treaty of Versailles. No demand was made to try Austrian war leaders, and reparations were limited to what Austria could afford to pay, which was nothing. Austria was not obliged to liquidate its foreign assets, and loans were to be given to the new republic by the League of Nations, albeit at the cost of Austria's budgetary sovereignty. On the other hand, many documents and works of art having their origin in the Secessionist States and Italy were removed from the archives and galleries in Vienna. The Austrian army was limited to 30,000 men (compared to 35,000 for Hungary), but the government could have scarcely afforded a larger one. The Secessionist States rejected an Allied proposal to limit the size of their armies, since it would eliminate the distinction between "victors" and "vanquished."

Far more open to criticism was the manner in which the Allies justified their handiwork. The Treaty of St. Germain, like the other Paris treaties, was supposed to be founded upon general principles of justice. Yet the German Austrians (and the Magyars) were held accountable for reparations because they, along with the Germans, had allegedly been exclusively responsible for starting the war. The Viennese, moreover, were accused

of acclaiming the war at its outbreak. The frontiers with Czechoslovakia were defended on the ground that "in the course of the
last one hundred years the Czech nation was little by little dispossessed of the rights which had been granted it by a long series
of formal documents, imperial rescripts, or decisions of the
sovereign diets."[8]

The Allies thus swallowed the arguments of the *emigré*
politicians hook, line, and sinker. The Austrians were able to
point out that no Alpine German had ever been a foreign minister during the Dualistic era and that the German Austrians
had been a minority in the Reichsrat after 1907. Historians
in the Allied countries themselves soon proved that the Central
Powers were by no means solely responsible for the war. And if
the war was acclaimed in Vienna, so too was it in Prague, Cra-
cow, Zagreb, Belgrade, and Paris and all the other belligerent
capitals of Europe. As for the Czechs, far from losing their rights
during the nineteenth century, they had gained nearly full political, economic, and cultural equality. In thus playing historians,
the Allies gratuitously added insult to the already serious injury
of the peace treaty.

The Austrian people had been prepared for a hard peace,
but St. Germain came as a brutal shock. They had hoped that
the elimination of the dynasty and the old army would produce
reasonable terms. When these expectations were disappointed,
the Socialists, who had led the fight against monarchism and
militarism, were held responsible by their rivals, just as their
counterparts were in Germany.

Hungary at the Peace Conference

The treatment of Austria in the Treaty of St. Germain was
mild compared to that handed out to Hungary. The Hungarians
were not invited to Paris until December 1, 1919, after Béla Kun's
Bolshevik government had been replaced by the ultraconserva-

---

[8] *FRUS, PPC*, vol. VII, *Reply of the Allied and Associated Powers to the Re-
marks of the Austrian Delegation of the Conditions of Peace*, p. 865.

tive regime of the Regent, Admiral Miklós Horthy. When the Hungarians arrived in the French capital all territorial questions involving their country had been decided. Well over 3 million Magyars had been placed under foreign domination: close to 1 million in Czechoslovakia, 1.7 million in Rumania, and nearly 470,000 in Yugoslavia. Some of them, such as 600,000 "Szekelys" in eastern Transylvania, were far removed from the Hungarian heartland and could have been incorporated in the new Hungary only by including an equal number of Rumanians. About 1.5 million Magyars, however, lived in compact blocks just beyond the Trianon frontiers.

Several principles were used in deciding Hungary's new borders. Areas with three or more nationalities were always assigned to Hungary's neighbors if they had non-Magyar majorities, even when the recipient state had an even smaller plurality of nationals than Hungary. Third nationalities such as the Ruthenes or Germans were assumed to prefer non-Hungarian rule. Mixed Magyar-Rumanian districts were given to Rumania because the Rumanians held a majority in the countryside, but 250,000 rural Magyars were transferred to Yugoslavia since 100,000 Serbs lived in the city of Subotica.

Allied treatment of the Hungarian peace delegation in Paris was no better than that given the Austrians. The Hungarians were isolated, and their communications with Budapest were restricted. The strategy pursued by the Hungarians, on the other hand, was in marked contrast to that followed by the Austrians. The latter based their case on the ethnic principle; the Hungarians asked for nothing less than the maintenance of their country's historic boundaries. The demand was extravagant given the political situation of 1920, although in principle it was no more illogical than the Czech demand for Bohemia's historic frontiers.

The Hungarian delegation backed its position with a barrage of historic, geographic, and economic information; but it was a wasted effort. Whereas the Allies had given detailed replies and made fairly substantial concessions to Germany's many objections to the Treaty of Versailles, they gave only a perfunctory answer to the Hungarian complaints and made almost no territorial concessions. The request for plebiscites in the severed territories was rejected (except for one small section of German West Hungary) on the ground that "such a consultation . . . would not offer a result differing sensibly from those which they [the Allies] have arrived after a minute study of the ethnographic conditions of Central Europe and of national aspirations. . . ."[9]

Privately, the Allies were no longer so sure about the justice of the Hungarian boundaries. But now it was too late to go back. The newly formed "Little Entente" of Czechoslovakia, Rumania, and Yugoslavia made it clear that it would accept no plebiscites, even under neutral supervision, and reminded the Allied Conference of Ambassadors and Foreign Ministers that the Supreme Council had informed the Little Entente states on several occasions that their boundaries were final. Their new frontiers had also been sanctioned by President Wilson. The Allies realized that to alter them in Hungary's favor now could only be accomplished by force, a measure they had neither the desire nor perhaps the means to employ.

Trianon thus had the dubious honor of being the most drastic of the Paris treaties. Not even Brest Litovsk, which had been repeatedly denounced by the Allies, could match the severity of the Treaty of Trianon. Russia was slated to lose a third of its population, but few if any Great Russians. The new Hungary, by contrast, was left with only 37 percent of its prewar population (or a little less than 8 million) and 28 percent of its prewar territory (or less than 36,000 square miles). No fewer than a third of all the Magyar people were turned over to foreign rule. Rumania alone acquired more of the old Hungary than did Hungary itself.

The Hungarian people doubtless would have been embittered initially by almost any loss of territory; but their eventual acceptance of the loss of German West Hungary indicates their ability to reconcile themselves to a just settlement. No patriotic Hungarian, however, could accept Trianon as final. Revision

[9] Quoted in Francis Deak, *Hungary at the Paris Peace Conference* (New York: Columbia University Press, 1942), p. 279.

of the treaty (or simply "revisionism") became almost an obsession with the Hungarian people and their government throughout the interwar period.

The Emergence of Yugoslavia, Greater Rumania, and Poland

Hungary's neighbors, either combined or alone, had little
to fear from Hungarian revisionism so long as no great power
was willing to back Hungary's claims with military support.
All of the states bordering Hungary, with the exception of Austria, were far greater in territory, population, and natural resources.

Hungary's neighbor to the south, Yugoslavia, had over
96,000 square miles and 12 million people, both figures being
about three times greater than comparable ones for the old Kingdom of Serbia. The Kingdom of the Serbs, Croats, and Slovenes,
as it was officially called until 1929, was somewhat less fortunate
than the other Secessionist States, since it lost over 700,000 nationals, 480,000 of them to Italy, and was left without satisfactory
port facilities. On the other hand, Yugoslavia acquired nearly
500,000 Magyars, over 500,000 Germans, and 230,000 Rumanians.
The country was therefore placed in the anomalous position of
being both an irredentist and a *status quo* power. With all but
one of its seven neighbors, it had border disputes, Greece being
the unimportant exception. Far more serious than any of these
quarrels, however, was the disaffection of the 3.5 million Croatians who regarded the Serbs not as liberators, but as con-
querors and oppressors.

The Rumanian delegation left Paris with even fewer disap-
pointments than the Yugoslavs. Its prewar area of less than
54,000 square miles containing 7.5 million people had mush-
roomed to nearly 114,000 square miles with 16 million inhabitants. Although the Italians and French had affirmed the validity
of the secret Treaty of Bucharest which brought Rumania into
the war in 1916, Rumania's western frontier fell somewhat short
of wartime promises. But this loss was more than compensated
for by the addition of 17,000 square miles in Bessarabia, taken

from Russia during its civil war, and 1000 square miles acquired in southern Bucovina.

Of all the Secessionist States, with the possible exception of Czechoslovakia, Poland's international and domestic status was the most dangerous. For the Poles, nothing failed like success. They gained their outlet to the Baltic through the so-called Polish Corridor. They annexed Prussian Upper Silesia, with its valuable industries and mineral deposits, and they conquered great stretches of land from the Bolsheviks in the Polish-Russian war. Pilsudski's aim, sensibly enough, was so to diminish the size of the Soviet Union that a new European balance of power would emerge. But the war ended with the compromise Treaty of Riga (March 1921), and Poland thereby added Russia's undying hatred to Germany's. And the failure of the West to give Poland all-out support against the Bolsheviks created in the Poles the illusion that they could defend themselves if necessary without foreign assistance. The compromise nature of the Treaty of Riga with Russia, which divided the White Russians and Ukrainians between the two belligerents, meant that Poland, only 65 percent Polish, would resemble Czechoslovakia in being a multinational state with a nation-state ideology.

If Poland was neither a multinational federal state nor a homogeneous nation-state, its 150,000 square miles and over 27 million people also meant that it was too large to play the passive role of a small state, but was not strong enough to qualify as a truly great power. Its ambiguous domestic and international condition was to plague Poland throughout the interwar period and contribute substantially to its eventual destruction.

The New Minorities and Ethnic Justice

In 1929 Winston Churchill, in an oft-quoted passage, cheerfully observed that "all the disputable areas put together were but a minute fraction of Europe. . . . Probably less than three percent of the European population are now living under Governments whose nationality they repudiate."[10] Churchill

---

[10] *The World Crisis: The Aftermath* (New York: Scribner, 1929), p. 211.

never explained how he arrived at that calculation; the actual count was at least 5 percent. Regardless of the figure for the whole of Europe, however, it would ignore the sensitive area between Russia and Germany, stretching from Finland to Greece, where no less than 20 to 25 percent of the population consisted of national minorities. And if dissatisfied people like the Austrians, Slovaks, and Croatians were included, the figure would be around 33 percent.

The Peace Conference was not unaware of the existence of the minorities, or of their possible threat to international peace. To compensate for their lack of self-determination, they were placed under the protection of "minority treaties" guaranteed by the League of Nations. But in practice, the treaties were unenforceable, and even resented by most of the states obliged to sign them.

Minority rights could have been protected far better through an equal distribution of national minorities among the Successor States. If this had been done, every minority would have acted as a hostage for the humane treatment of minorities elsewhere. Voluntary exchanges might have been feasible and international cooperation rendered more likely. As it was, the treaties left Austria and Hungary with no bargaining power and the Secessionist States with little reason to make concessions. In many cases the distribution of minorities was grotesque. Rumania was given 1.7 million Magyars, while Hungary received 25,000 Rumanians. Three and a quarter million German Austrians were left in Czechoslovakia compared to 100,000 Czechs in Austria. Italy acquired 480,000 Yugoslavs, while Yugoslavia obtained 9,500 Italians.

Impartiality was not practiced in Paris because the Allies regarded the Secessionist States as the victors, while Austria and Hungary were still seen as the vanquished. Actually, the Secessionist States had little to do with the Allied victory, and only the Czechs could legitimately claim a political tradition in harmony with the Western democracies. With the exception of the Czechs and possibly the Poles, the Secessionist States were no more the natural allies of the West than the Austrians or Hungarians. The latter two had never considered Britain,

France, or the United States to be their enemies in any meaningful sense. At the end of the war Wilsonianism was as popular in Vienna and Budapest as elsewhere in East Central Europe. The Austrians and Hungarians, as we have seen, expected to make heavy sacrifices and could have adjusted to treaties giving them self-determination.

The Allies were therefore not faced with the painful choice of satisfying some states at the expense of totally alienating others. Taaffe's formula of "well balanced discontent" would have been the happiest solution. But by deliberately favoring the Secessionist States the Allies lost the possible friendship of Austria and Hungary. With characteristic shrewdness, Charles Seymour, one of the American experts at Paris, noted in a private letter that

> everything that has been done in Paris has tended to force Austria into the arms of Germany. A little more tact and diplomatic skill and Austria could have been kept absolutely free from German influence. . . . A really wise policy would have been to place German Austria on the same plane as Jugoslavia and Czechoslovakia — not regarding it as an enemy state — but this would have been a policy demanding more foresight and intelligence than anybody connected with the French Foreign Office possesses.[11]

Only the British delegation agreed with Seymour's view.

Principles Behind the Treaties

Self-determination was the principle behind the Allied encouragement of Austria-Hungary's disintegration; but the theory was only imperfectly applied at Paris. It was specifically denied to the German Austrians, and no one bothered to ascertain the real wishes of the Slovaks, Ruthenes, Croatians, or most of the Slovenes. In the few cases where plebiscites were held, the results often contradicted the national doctrine. Many Carinthian Slovenes voted for Austria, not Yugoslavia. Poles in

[11] Charles Seymour and Harold B. Whiteman, Jr. (ed.), *Letters from the Paris Peace Conference* edited by Harold B. Whiteman, Jr. (New Haven, Conn.: Yale University Press, 1965), p. 268.

southern East Prussia voted overwhelmingly for Germany, not Poland. Where two or three nationalities spoke related Slavic languages, it was simply taken for granted that they wanted to live in the same state, even if they had a long history of animosity.

These assumptions had more in common with racism (as the word was then used) than self-determination. A middle-class Styrian Slovene was felt to have more in common with a Macedonian peasant who had lived under Turkish rule for five centuries than with a German-speaking fellow Styrian. A Slovak peasant was said to have an identity of interest with a sophisticated, secularized Czech from Prague, but not with a Magyar peasant next door with whom he shared a thousand-year historical tradition.

Interestingly enough, none other than Woodrow Wilson became somewhat disillusioned with the self-determination principle even before the signing of the Treaty of Versailles. In June 1919 he told an American delegate to the Peace Conference who was promoting Irish independence that

> 'When I gave utterance to those words ["self-determination"], I said them without the knowledge that nationalities existed which are coming to us day after day. . . . You do not know and cannot appreciate the anxieties I have experienced as the result of these many millions of peoples having their hopes raised by what I have said.' [Three months later Wilson clarified his meaning:] 'It is not within the privilege of the conference of peace to act upon the right of self-determination of any peoples except those which had been included in the defeated empires.'[12]

Although self-determination ignored history, the historic principle was nevertheless sometimes utilized in determining boundaries. Italy claimed the South Tyrol, since it had belonged to Italy during the Roman Empire. The Czechs appealed to the historic unity of the Bohemian crownlands, and the Poles tried to restore the Poland of 1772. No account, however, was given to the historical development of the Habsburg Monarchy since

---

[12] Quoted in Louis Gerson, *The Hyphenate in Recent American Politics and Diplomacy* (Lawrence, Kan.: University of Kansas Press, 1964), pp. 82–83.

1526 or the thousand-year history of the Hungarian kingdom. History was also set aside in determining the southern boundaries of Carinthia and Styria.

Economic needs were often considered, as they were when Czechoslovakia was given the Danube port of Bratislava and a strip of the Hungarian plain facilitating east-west communications. But Austria's needs for north-south transport in Burgenland and east-west transit through Carinthia, Styria, and the Tyrol were ignored. The same was true of Hungary's need for the forests, waterpower, and minerals of Ruthenia and Transylvania.

Strategic factors also played a major role at Paris: Italy received the Brenner Pass; Czechoslovakia was given the Sudeten mountains and a portion of the Danube River; Yugoslavia got a wide section of southern Hungary, and Rumania a belt of territory in eastern Hungary. With the exception of the Sudeten frontier, however, it was always the strong who received protection against the weak. Paradoxically, the strategic frontiers, involving the annexation of countless minorities, only produced a sense of insecurity. "The war to end all wars" was in fact followed by feverish preparations for the next one.

It was France which was determined that prospective allies in East Central Europe be given strategic frontiers. The result perverted the idealism of the Conference. Lansing and Lloyd George viewed the French policy with suspicion, but lacked the determination and realistic alternatives to block the fulfillment of the French objectives. Wilson interested himself only in the Italian-Yugoslav, Carinthian, and Polish-German boundaries of East Central Europe. Otherwise he gave his blessing to the Treaties of St. Germain and Trianon. Any possible injustices, he felt, could be corrected later by the League of Nations.

In Defense of the Treaties

However unjust the final peace terms may have appeared in the eyes of the Austrians and Hungarians, the peacemakers did at least limit the rapacity of the Secessionist States. Yugoslavia did not get Klagenfurt, Villach, or Radkersburg. Czechoslovakia was denied certain small areas in Lower Austria and much larger sections of what became northern Hungary; it also failed to gain a corridor to Yugoslavia. Neither Italy nor Rumania was given everything it had been promised in the secret treaties of London and Bucharest. Reparations were limited in practice to what Austria and Hungary could afford to pay, and the Secessionist States had to share in repaying the debts of the Dual Monarchy. Food was rushed to Austria and Hungary, and both countries were allowed immediate entry into the League of Nations, where they were given substantial loans. Contrary to the charges of revisionist historians, the treaty makers, for the most part, did not make their decisions in ignorance of ethnic, geographic, or economic facts. If anything they were overburdened with technical information. No doubt popular passions also made it more difficult for the peacemakers to draw up a perfectly impartial settlement, although it is hard to agree with Nicolson that "Clemenceau . . . would . . . have been hurled from power" if he had permitted a few hundred thousand more German-Austrians and Magyars to remain in Austria and Hungary.[13] To paraphrase what the British representative wrote about Wilson and the South Tyrol, if the French could swallow Clemenceau's failure to obtain the Rhineland, they would swallow anything.

Finally, it is too often forgotten that not all the problems of the interwar period can be attributed to the treaties. Serious political, economic, social, and moral dilemmas existed in Europe, particularly in East Central Europe, before the war. Four years of desperate fighting magnified those conditions. No treaty maker could wave a magic wand and make them disappear.

Chaos Along the Danube

On the negative side, the outstanding moral and political defect of the treaties was their denial of self-determination to most of the German- and many of the Magyar-speaking inhabi-

---

[13] Nicolson, *op. cit.*, p. 89.

tants of the old Monarchy. The psychological consequences of imposed independence for the Republic of Austria were utterly demoralizing. By renouncing the dynasty the Austrians were consciously attempting to make a clean break with the past and to begin a new national existence. The Allies made this well-nigh impossible by insisting that the new Austria was the legal and moral heir of the old Monarchy. They even demanded that Alpine Germans call their country "Austria" instead of the "German Austria" chosen by the National Assembly.

The Republic of Austria actually had many advantages not possessed by most other Successor States. It had not been a battlefield during the war; it was well endowed with industry and waterpower, and had a landscape likely to produce a flourishing tourist industry. It was by far the most ethnically homogeneous of the Successor States, and had citizens with great technical skills and artistic talent. The economic history of the Second Austrian Republic has demonstrated that the nonviability of the First Republic was largely a myth. It was therefore not material conditions but the sense of hopelessness and moral depression which made the First Republic unworkable. In favoring the exaggerated claims of Italy, Yugoslavia, and Czechoslovakia, the Allies contributed to the conviction that union with Germany was Austria's only hope for survival.

No one should be surprised that the Allies rejected the *Anschluss* solution for both Austria and the Sudetenland. Versailles Germany had 62 million people compared to 39 million in France. To have added 10 million German Austrians to the Reich's population would have made the Franco-German disparity even more lopsided. The dilemma was apparently insoluble, but only apparently. Robert Lansing, as well as a great many Bavarians, favored the creation of an independent south German state. An early proponent of breaking up the Monarchy, the American Secretary of State soon feared that the phrase "self-determination" was "loaded with dynamite," and was likely to "raise hopes which could never be realized."[14] He now deplored the replacement of Austria-Hungary by a

---

[14] Quoted in Gerson, *op. cit.*, p. 76.

"mass of small covetous and quarrelsome nations," and concluded that "wars are by no means over."[15]

Lansing's worst fears might have gone unrealized had an
independent south German state been created out of Bavaria,
Austria, the Sudetenland, and possibly Baden, and Württem-
berg. Such a state, with a population of 22 million, would have
fulfilled the south German desire for separation from Prussia;
the Austrians would have been able to join other Germans;
and the Sudeten Germans would have escaped a hated alien
rule. The seriousness of Czechoslovakia's minority problem
would have been substantially diminished, and Germany's
population would have been reduced by some 13 million, making what remained less of a threat to France, Czechoslovakia,
and Poland. Under these circumstances the Allies would have
been less concerned about Germany's reparations and disarma-
ment. If an *Anschluss* movement had developed in the new
state, its intensity most certainly would have been feeble compared to the movement that actually arose in Austria and the
Sudetenland after 1918. At worst, a north-south German reunion
could have had consequences no more serious than those following the events of 1938. That Lansing's idea was never imple-
mented was probably due to the strength of the nation-state
ideology and the unpopularity of the balance of power concept.
Perhaps the Allies were also afraid that such a drastic decision
would enrage the Prussians. In a more mundane way it may have
resulted from the friction between Wilson and Lansing because
of the latter's lack of enthusiasm for the League of Nations,
which he regarded as "an instrument of the mighty."[16]

The Peace Settlement in East Central Europe, instead of
realizing Wilson's dream of self-determination, was a compromise between the Franco-Italian quest for security and the
Anglo-American concern for justice. But the one-sided use of

[15] Quoted in Dagmar H. Perman, *The Shaping of the Czechoslovak State: Diplomatic History of the Boundaries of Czechoslovakia* (Leiden: E. J. Brill, 1962),
p. 205.
[16] *FRUS, PPC*, vol. XI, *Memorandum by the Secretary of State, Paris,* May 8,
1919, p. 568.

nonethnic criteria to establish boundaries created injustices, and the injustices created insecurity. So many contradictory principles were employed in drawing up the treaties of St. Germain and Trianon that the final product looked as if the world had been made "safe for hypocracy."[17] Abused ideals have a tremendous potentiality for vengeance. A major difficulty during the interwar period in arousing popular support for the forceful maintenance of the Paris Settlement was the weakness of the intellectual and moral foundations of the peace.

The Paris treaties were harsh enough to cause nationalists in the West to gloat and liberals to wring their hands in dismay. Both reactions supplied useful ammunition for Central European revisionists. Further, by dividing the Successor States into victors and vanquished the Allies aggravated rather than appeased national hatreds. National rivalries that had been domestic before the war were now internationalized, and the likelihood of war was increased.

One part of Central Europe was still united: Germany. It was also the real beneficiary of the Danubian chaos. Before the war it had been bordered on the east and south by two great powers. In their place were now four small and weak states harboring millions of outraged Germans. A ready-made fifth column awaited Adolf Hitler.

The chaotic state of East Central Europe after 1918 was the result of one basic mistake: the failure of the Big Four to work out a general plan for a postwar settlement. Only the French had thought out a strategy and it was simple: to reward their "friends" (i.e., the Secessionist States) and punish their enemies, Austria and Hungary. Italy was out to get all the territory it could and to strengthen the neighbors of its new rival, Yugoslavia. The only plan possessed by the United States (and it was generally supported by the British) consisted of Wilson's extremely vague Fourteen Points and Four Principles. Wilson did not even define what he meant by "self-determination." The American commissioners were at a loss as to what they should fight for. During

[17] E. J. Dillon, *The Inside Story of the Peace Conference* (New York: Harper and Brothers, 1920), p. 116.

the war the President had opposed any discussion of war aims, even with the British, for fear it would cause misunderstandings that would hinder the war effort.

The extreme nationalism of the late nineteenth century had not produced a statesman after Bismarck with the ability to see international questions in an all-European context. No Castlereagh or Metternich could be found at Paris in 1919. The twentieth-century peacemakers admittedly faced problems even more overwhelming than those of 1814–1815. National and social unrest was comparatively unknown in the early nineteenth century, and political institutions and the men who ran them were not seriously challenged. The world of 1919, on the other hand, was far more revolutionary and insecure. Still, the Big Four, as elderly men of the nineteenth century, were too willing to rely on the nineteenth-century doctrines of liberal nationalism and laissez-faire economics. Events in East Central Europe in 1918–1919 were therefore allowed to take their natural course. The Allies, or at any rate Britain and the United States, did not take the middle zone between Germany and Russia seriously. Germany and Bolshevism were still the only important problems. Other areas and issues could be safely allowed to take care of themselves.

CHAPTER FOUR

The
Democratic
Interlude
1920–1933

The Failure of Democratic Institutions

In 1919 the new democratic institutions of
East Central Europe were hailed throughout the
Western world as some of the greatest by-products
of the Allied victory. Fourteen years later only
Czechoslovakia could still boast free institutions,
and even there democracy was not the unqualified
success imagined by admirers in the West. What
went wrong?

Certain problems were common to all or most
of the Successor States. Resistance to the dictatorial
wartime governments of Austria-Hungary, Russia,
and Germany undermined the prestige of all established authority. In postwar Austria, the provinces felt no sense of loyalty to the Vienna government now that the Habsburgs were gone. National
minorities in the Secessionist States were even less

willing to submit to governments that had annexed them. Fearing for the integrity of their boundaries, Secessionist States reacted to the minority danger by adopting highly centralized constitutions. The new constitutions only exacerbated the minority problem and alienated even peoples of state such as the Slovaks, Croatians, and Slovenes.

Proportional representation was supposed to compensate for the absence of regional government. As in the voting arrangement used for the Austrian Reichsrat after 1907, the system guaranteed every political party representation equal to its percentage of votes in the last election. Nearly every nationality and ideological faction was thereby theoretically assured a voice in national affairs. Unfortunately, the setup worked no better after 1918 than it had in prewar Austria. Political cleavages were emphasized. The Polish Sejm (Parliament) was like a pen full of hungry dogs with fifteen parties fighting over political bones. The Czechoslovak parliamentary elections of 1920 were contested by no fewer than 23 political parties with 8 Czech and Slovak, 6 German, and 3 Magyar parties gaining representation. Twelve parties competed in the Yugoslav Skupstina, while the Rumanian lower house contained so many factions as to defy precise enumeration. The formation of stable ministries everywhere thus became a near impossibility.

All of the Successor States had problems of one kind or another arising from their bureaucracies. The new or greatly enlarged countries required costly civil, foreign, and military services; Austria and Hungary had to absorb an enormous bureaucratic surplus in their rump territories. The civil service systems, along with the educational institutions of the Austro-Hungarian Monarchy, were transferred to the Successor States. But difficulties arose in countries where two or more administrative traditions were inherited. The Historic Provinces of Czechoslovakia, for example, retained Austrian practices which were then imposed in Slovak and Ruthene districts accustomed to less efficient Hungarian ways. In Rumania, Poland, and Yugoslavia it was the oppressive and sometimes brutal systems of the Regat, Russian Poland, and Serbia which predominated in a process known as "Balkanization." Minority nationali in all the Successor States soon found themselves underrepresented in the civil services, if indeed they were represented at all.

In addition to the nearly universal difficulties arising from new constitutions and new bureaucracies, each of the Successor States had special problems of its own. In Austria, party divisions went deeper than was healthy for a democratic society. The capital, now a province in its own right, was securely controlled by the Social Democratic party, the provinces by the Christian Social party. Marxists opposed Catholics; rural districts were set against "Red" Vienna.

Austria was typical of the Successor States in passing through a brief period of Socialist predominance which in its case lasted until the breakup of the coalition government in 1920. Reacting against the authoritarian powers of the Habsburgs, Socialists not only in Austria, but all over East Central Europe, demanded that executive powers be severely restricted. The Austrian Constitution of 1920 therefore prevented both the chancellor and the president from dissolving the National Assembly. As a consequence, Austrian ministries found it almost impossible to pursue strong and consistent policies unhampered by party politics. Austrian democracy was therefore weakened from the beginning by the ineffectiveness of the government.

Austria was unique in not having a multiparty system. With few national minorities, party politics revolved entirely around ideological and social issues. Not needing to unite against common internal or external enemies, the two major parties and the smaller "Pan-German People's party" glared at one another with ill-disguised contempt.

The Social Democrats, the most powerful Marxist party outs⋯ ⋯e Soviet Union, succeeded in holding most leftists ⋯ ⋯le organization; the Austrian Communists remained ⋯ small splinter group. But Socialist unity came ⋯ Left-wing radicals were pacified with verbal ⋯m of Marxist jargon advocating the creation ⋯tate for the benefit of the proletariat. In ⋯rk was far worse than their bite; but ⋯m alienated many a potential bour-⋯ end of the First Republic, Socialists could never decide between their moderation in practical affairs and their ideological radicalism. Not surprisingly, they succeeded neither in conciliating their rivals nor in eliminating them by revolutionary means. And their insistence that they were the only true democrats pushed many anti-Socialists into the antidemocratic camp. The victory for party unity was a defeat for Austrian democracy. Antidemocratic feelings were especially prevalent among right-wing members of the Christian Social party who were unenthusiastic about the Republic from the outset. The Roman Catholic Church had enjoyed a privileged position in the Monarchy, and believers feared with reason that the Republic would encourage secularism.

The cleavage between Left and Right in Austrian politics was made all the deeper by a personal feud between party leaders. The left-wing Socialist Otto Bauer took control of his party following the resignation of the moderate, Karl Renner from the chancellorship. Jewish and a brilliant theoretician, Bauer stood poles apart ideologically from Monsignor Ignaz Seipel, the authoritarian, humorless, and austere priest-politician (popularly known as "Autrichlieu," the Austrian Richelieu), who served as chancellor from 1922 to 1924 and again from 1926 to 1929. For Seipel, Marxism was the mortal enemy of Christianity and the Church. For Bauer, the Church was the principal obstacle to progress. Bauer was a Marxist first and an Austrian second; Seipel was first a Catholic, then an Austrian. In the eyes of their enemies the one was a "revolutionary," the other a "reactionary." As long as these men were ascendant, opportunities for cooperation between the two major parties were minimal.

But it is doubtful whether democracy in the Austrian Republic ever had much of a chance. On the fundamental questions of social welfare, church-state relations, and later the *Anschluss,* the three political factions could reach no agreement. Extremists saw their rivals, not as honest if mistaken men, but as heretics to be eliminated one way or another. Private armies were even organized: the *Schutzbund* (Defense League) for Socialists, the *Heimwehr* (Home Guard) for conservatives.

The *Heimwehr* originated in 1918 as a defense force

against domestic Communists and Yugoslavs threatening the southern frontier. After a Socialist uprising in Vienna in 1927 the *Heimwehr* became more aggressive and exclusively devoted to the extermination of Marxism in all its forms. Its leadership was drawn from the professional middle class, the group hardest hit by the breakup of the Monarchy and most fearful of a proletarian revolution. The *Heimwehr's* attempt to unify the country under a fascist banner met with little success, since it had no charismatic leader or constructive program. In the end its only achievements were the further discrediting of democracy and the prevention of a possible reconciliation between Marxists and Catholics.

Politics was less partisan and doctrinaire in Czechoslovakia than in Austria, although Czechoslovakia resembled its southern neighbor in lacking constructive opposition parties. Parties outside the Czech ministry not only objected to the government, but also to the very existence of the state. The five Czech coalition parties nearly always confronted a solid opposition. The power of the government parties was so unshakable that they came to think of it as a natural right. And Communists and national minorities, permanently out of office, failed to develop unified or positive programs.

The isolation of the Czech political parties was actually of some value, as they were faced with the stark necessity of forming a unified front against common internal and external enemies, a habit already cultivated during their participation in the Austrian Reichsrat. Unlike postwar Austrians, the Czechs could not afford the luxury of internal divisions.

But the greatest difference between political life in Czechoslovakia and that in Austria lay in the leadership of Thomas Masaryk and Edvard Beneš. Masaryk was already an elder statesman and "father" of his country when he took over the Czech presidency in 1918. As a secular, liberal-nationalist, he was the antithesis of Franz Joseph, whose empire he helped to destroy. Yet in some respects the two men were strangely alike. Both reached the peak of their popularity late in life and died at almost identical ages. Both were able to stand above partisan politics and reconcile (to some extent at least) quarreling fac-

Thomas G. Masaryk (1850–1937), president of Czechoslovakia, 1918–1935. *(Culver Pictures)*

tions. Neither was adverse to appointing cabinets of experts, rather than politicians, if the needs of state demanded it. By an odd coincidence, both died two years before the disintegration of their states.

The reaction against monarchical rule did not limit Masaryk's formal powers to the same extent as was true of chief executives in other Successor States. He had the right to appoint cabinet ministers and other high state officials as well as to negotiate international treaties. His real power, however, rested on his unequaled personal prestige and popularity, which he used to provide Czech domestic politics with a firm element of stability during his long administration (1918–1935). A similar consistency was provided in foreign affairs by Beneš. Czech cabinets came and went with monotonous frequency, but the foreign minister remained the same. Even when he was elevated to the presidency in 1935, Beneš retained control over foreign affairs.

The political problems of Yugoslavia were not unlike those of Czechoslovakia. But the South Slavs lacked an educated, liberal middle class to cope with them. Both the Czechs and Serbs attempted to impose their institutions and political philosophy on hostile nationalities. The more tactful Czechs, however, managed to gain, for a time at least, the sullen cooperation of the national minorities and Slovaks; the Serbs encountered only stubborn resistance.

The central issue in Yugoslav politics was the constitutional structure of the state. The prewar Magyar-Croatian feud was simply transplanted to Yugoslavia. Serbs could never overcome their conviction that they had "liberated" the other South Slavs and therefore assumed that the liberated nationalities ought to be ruled as though they were extensions of the prewar Serbian kingdom. This notion was incorporated into the Yugoslav constitution. Adopted during a boycott of the Croatian parties, it did little more than revive the prewar Serbian constitution. The Serbs, with a literacy rate of less than 50 percent, were thus granted the constitutional right to rule a state three times the size of their old kingdom.

Croatians and Slovenes considered their association with

the Serbs to be strictly voluntary and expected at least as much local autonomy as they had enjoyed under Austro-Hungarian rule. Instead, local officials, particularly in Croatia, received orders directly from Belgrade ministries having little respect for regional peculiarities. Slovenes fared considerably better, since their distinct language protected them from possible encroachment by the Serbian bureaucracy. The superiority of their educational institutions even led to overrepresentation in national agencies. The highest government offices, however, were nearly always staffed by Serbs.

A constitutional crisis in Yugoslav politics was reached in June 1928 when a Montenegrin parliamentary deputy fatally wounded the leader of the Croat Peasant party, Stjepan Radić. Radić's party immediately seceded from Parliament, and in January 1929 King Alexander suspended the constitution initiating a royal dictatorship that lasted until his murder in 1934. In an attempt to break down regional loyalties, the historic provinces were replaced by new administrative districts ignoring history and nationality. Nothing worked. Government was just as unstable as before; regionalism was undiminished; and assassinations were the order of the day. Even the Serbs, who continued to hold the top official positions, grew impatient with the prolonged denial of civil liberties; but a new constitution promulgated by the king in 1931 failed to restore individual rights. In an attempt to reduce factionalism it sharply reduced the importance of parliamentary bodies and eliminated proportional representation; the king retained the right to appoint and dismiss the prime minister and all members of the cabinet. Even these measures, however, failed to renew, or rather create, Yugoslav unity.

National strife, which tore apart Czechoslovakia and Yugoslavia, was almost entirely absent in postwar Hungary. The staggering loss of territory, together with the excesses of the Béla Kun regime, united the Hungarian people in a common passion for territorial revision and anti-Communism. Kun had carried out an "anti-God" campaign and capped it by a reign of terror against all opposition. Not only Bolshevism but also republicanism had been brought under a cloud. The monarchy was restored almost by default, although resolute opposition from the Little Entente twice prevented a return of the Habsburgs.

Hungary received a bad press in the Western democracies between the wars. Whereas Czechoslovakia and other Secessionist States were held up as models of democracy, Hungary was the reactionary, warmongering whipping boy. Only part of the criticism was deserved. The prewar constitution was restored and the franchise was limited to 27 percent of the population. The open ballot returned in rural districts until 1938, facilitating bribery and blackmail, and making badly needed reforms even harder to advocate. The old landed oligarchy regained both political and economic power after Kun's ouster.

But not all aspects of the new Hungary represented black reaction. Although there was a Government party with a constant parliamentary majority, other parties, including Socialists, were tolerated. If the Head of State and. Regent, Admiral Miklós Horthy, could dissolve Parliament at will and select a minister-president of his own choosing, he was also careful not to exceed his constitutional authority or establish himself as dictator.

Strikingly handsome, the Regent inspired great affection from those who knew him well. He was honest, courteous, and generous, and had a model family life although one touched by several tragedies. An archconservative who strove to regain Hungary's historic frontiers, he also doggedly resisted the temptation to make his country a Nazi satellite to achieve this goal. In the end, his overthrow came from the far Right, not from the Left. Thanks largely to Horthy's integrity and the solidarity of the Magyar people, Hungary, easily the least democratic of the Successor States in 1920, was the only one that preserved some semblance of democracy and constitutional rights twenty years later.

Poland's political life was a composite of elements found elsewhere in East Central Europe. The Constitution of 1921 resembled Austria's in creating an all-powerful Parliament that could not be dissolved by the executive. Like Czechoslovakia and Yugoslavia, Poland had a multiparty system, but unlike the Czechs, the Poles were unable to make it work effectively. Between 1918 and 1926 no fewer than seventeen cabinet crises disrupted political life. As in Austria, deep ideological differences separated the parties, but in Poland the conservative, authoritarian, and clerical National Democratic party excluded the revolutionary Socialist party from power, whereas in Austria Socialist abstention until 1933 was usually voluntary.

Polish politics was dominated during most of the interwar period by the imposing figure of Marshal Józef Pilsudski. Born in the Russian part of Poland in 1867, Pilsudski became an irreconcilable enemy of the tsars when he was banished to Siberia between 1887 and 1892 for revolutionary activity. In the early years of the twentieth century he escaped another arrest and fled to Austrian Galicia, where he organized Polish students for possible military action against Russia. During the First World War he volunteered for service in the Austro-Hungarian army on the Russian front. No sooner had the Great War ended than Pilsudski was leading a Polish army against the Russian Bolsheviks. By 1920 he was unequaled as a national hero.

Pilsudski's political creed is something of a mystery. As a youthful revolutionary he had a motley collection of socialist ideas which as late as the early postwar years sufficed to attract a following in Leftist circles. As one of the principal founders of a resuscitated Poland he wisely hoped to create a federal state, although he never developed a practical federal program. The nationalistic and unitary theories of his opponents prevailed instead, and Poland lost an excellent opportunity to win over its Ukrainian and White Russian minorities.

Deep down, Pilsudski was a simple soldier whose only real ideology was militaristic and romantic nationalism. It was this belief in his country's greatness which induced him to resign his impotent presidential office in 1923. Disillusionment with the partisan politics of the Sejm during these early years led him to describe that body as "a sterile, jabbering, howling thing that engendered such boredom that the very flies on the walls died of sheer disgust."[1] He once admitted to a close friend that he

---

[1] Quoted in Gordon Craig, *Europe since 1914* (New York: Holt, Rinehart and Winston, 1966), p. 659.

was tempted to have one or two hundred of the scoundrelly deputies shot.

Pilsudski's retirement came to an early end in 1926 when he seized power by marching on Warsaw in a manner reminiscent of Mussolini's March on Rome four years earlier. The conviction that parliamentary government was incapable of dealing with political and economic distress caused him to regard strong leadership, which only he could provide, as the one possible solution to the crisis. The result was a real, if for a time somewhat disguised, dictatorship. While disdaining to fill the presidency to which he was elected, Pilsudski rotated by command fourteen cabinets in the nine years between his *coup* and his death in 1935. Parliamentary powers were sharply curtailed, and the president given the right of dissolution. In 1930 what amounted to a one-party system came into existence with only nominal opposition permitted. But with the help of foreign loans and the return of general European prosperity Pilsudski was able to give his homeland a measure of economic well-being. And his strong hand brought order to public administration and finance; it may have saved Poland from anarchy.

Complex is the best way of describing Pilsudski's character. Physically and morally courageous, energetic, hardworking, and punctual, he had few of the stereotyped Polish traits. He was also ruthless, erratic, and crude, even if he also had the patience and ability to unify disparate factions. Critics who were too outspoken, however, might find themselves arbitrarily imprisoned.

The complexity of Pilsudski's character is reflected in his political legacy. He hoped to establish a free, law-abiding, and pluralistic democracy by means of a *coup d'état*. He wanted to raise the prestige of the presidency, but refused to fill the office himself. Still another goal was to raise the respect and dignity of public officials, but he ridiculed members of Parliament unmercifully. No one can deny, however, that he did succeed in promoting Poland's international prestige and the self-confidence of the Polish people.

Pilsudski's death in 1935 removed a powerful centripetal force in Polish politics, a force comparable to Franz Joseph in prewar Austria. The dictatorship was continued and even strengthened constitutionally; but Pilsudski's military comrades who succeeded him were capable only of accumulating wealth and honors once his restraining influence was removed. When Poland faced the supreme test in 1939 the dictatorship was without a dictator.

Down on the Farm

The depressing fate of democracy in East Central Europe was matched by the area's dismal economic record. Agriculture was especially disappointing. It was easily the leading source of national income in nearly all the Successor States. Even in 1930, after a decade of frantic industrialization, 76 percent of the Yugoslavs, 72 percent of the Rumanians, 60 percent of the Poles, and 51 percent of the Hungarians were still dependent on agriculture. Only in Czechoslovakia (33 percent) and Austria (26 percent) did less than half the population till the soil. Nonetheless, agriculture remained the poor relation in the economic priorities of most governments, just as it is in most underdeveloped countries today. Peasants were given neither the technical knowledge nor the credit to modernize their farms. Productivity of wheat, for example, was only one-third to one-half that of Denmark. The already bleak conditions of the early postwar years were worsened by a rapid growth in population. Emigration, the traditional outlet for Europe's surplus population, came virtually to an end after the enactment of American immigration laws in 1921 and 1924. Industrialization was inadequate as a substitute outlet. Poland's population jumped from 27 to 35 million, Yugoslavia's from 12 to 16 million, and Rumania's from 16 to 20 million. Only Austria, Hungary, and Czechoslovakia were spared this explosion of births. Where peasants multiplied, the obvious result was an ever-diminishing amount of land for each family. Whereas there were only 36.6 people for every square kilometer of cultivable land in Denmark, the figure for Hungary was 80.6; Rumania, 116.3; and Yugoslavia, 157.4. In other words, Danubian peasants were able to grow only one-tenth to one-twelfth as much food as their Danish counterparts.

Most of the Successor States enacted land reform legislation. Trumpeted as a matter of elementary social justice, the reform was actually inspired at least as much by political and national considerations. Its usual consequence was to replace relatively efficient large estates with hopelessly unproductive small farms. But the large estates (except in Poland) had belonged to the old ruling nationalities—the German Austrians and the Magyars—whereas the new owners were Slavic peasants. The reforms succeeded in antagonizing the dispossessed minority nationalities, but failed to satisfy most peasants, who frequently found themselves more destitute in 1939 than they had been a quarter century before.

Austrian agriculture in 1918 appeared to be utterly inadequate for the needs of the country. Only one-fourth of all the land was arable, with a pathetic 4.5% consisting of plains. On the other hand, a mere tenth of the land was totally unproductive; the soil was reasonably fertile and the climate favorable for a variety of crops. Agricultural production was insufficient in 1919 partly because little effort had been made before the war to compete with the more productive farms of Bohemia and Hungary. With the help of tariffs, output increased to a point where in 1937 Austria was approaching self-sufficiency in certain basic foodstuffs. But the agricultural gains were paid for by higher food prices.

The key problem in Czechoslovak agriculture was land reform. The German-speaking aristocracy in the Historic Provinces and the Magyar proprietors of Slovakia and Ruthenia owned a relatively high percentage of the land in 1918. By one estimate, over one-quarter of Bohemia was owned by less than 2 percent of the landowners, while in Moravia one-third of the land was held by less than 1 percent of the landowners. Raw figures such as these, however, are misleading. Of the land held by the great noble families the greater part consisted of forests, whereas five-sixths of the actual farming land had been owned and cultivated by small farmers in 1914.

Land reform in Czechoslovakia, therefore, was necessarily less drastic than in places like Transylvania or northern Yugoslavia. Even landholders who had their land redistributed were allowed to retain 375 acres of arable land and 250 acres of forests, a sizable amount of property by European standards. And unlike the situation in other countries with land reforms in Czechoslovakia reform aided production; the country eventually produced about 90 percent of its food needs.

But the transparent political overtones of the reform could not fail to exacerbate hostile feelings between majority and minority nationalities. Compensation for great landholders amounted to only one-fifth the real value of their estates. Those owners who had displayed overt anti-Czech sympathies during the war received no compensation whatever. When the redistributed lands were turned over to Czechs and Slovaks, who settled in what had been purely German or Magyar districts, minorities saw the program as a deliberate effort to denationalize them.

Land reform was as good as nonexistent in Hungary, even though there was a staggering inequality of land distribution. But land owned by minorities was insignificant, and in Hungary, as elsewhere, the government had no desire to confiscate property belonging to the *Staatsvolk*. Other problems, in any case, were equally serious: rural overpopulation, overproduction, and low productivity. More than 60 percent of Trianon Hungary was suitable for plowing, and a mere 6.5 percent of the land had to be classified as unproductive. But gigantic territorial losses in the peace settlement had cost the country most of its minerals, forests, and waterpower, although it had left the best soil in the new Hungary while creating a better balance between industry and agriculture. In 1910, 64.5 percent of the population had been engaged in agriculture; ten years later the percentage was down to 55.8. Nevertheless, rural overpopulation was still enormous; 3 million peasants were virtually landless. Despite pathetically low productivity, the destruction of the Austro-Hungarian customs union made it difficult for Hungary to sell its huge agricultural surpluses. While trade was still comparatively free and food prices as high as they were during the twenties, Hungary was able to enjoy five years of prosperity. But the bottom fell out with the Great Depression of 1929 and the denunciation by Czechoslovakia of a trade agreement the following year.

The Industrial Scene

The dissolution of the Habsburg Monarchy had a relatively small impact on agriculture except for the shrinkage of internal markets. The central problem of rural overpopulation remained except where partially solved by land reform. Industry was another story, however. The boundaries laid down in Paris for East Central Europe gave little account to the relationship between raw materials, the factories that turned them into finished goods, or the consumers who were supposed to buy them.

Apart from industrial problems created by the breakup of the Monarchy were those related to postwar internal politics. Industries in Slovakia, for example, which had been heavily subsidized by the Hungarian government, were ignored by Prague after 1918. Industries in Serbia and the Regat received more favorable treatment in Belgrade and Bucharest than those in former Austro-Hungarian provinces. All of the Successor States, but especially the predominantly agricultural countries— Yugoslavia, Rumania, Poland, and Hungary—lacked native capital for industrial expansion. Foreign loans were fairly easy to obtain during the internationally tranquil twenties, but even then foreigners were inclined to invest their capital in industries bringing quick profits, not necessarily in those most needed locally. Then, with the coming of the Great Depression and the diplomatic instability of the thirties, almost all foreign investments came to a sudden end. Even industries built during the relatively prosperous twenties were wasteful, being paid for in part by peasants through taxes and prices for manufactured goods 50 percent to 300 percent higher than for prewar imports.

Overindustrialized Czechoslovakia and Austria were relatively unconcerned about the establishment of new factories. With only 25 percent of the inhabitants of the Austro-Hungarian Monarchy, Czechoslovakia inherited 86 percent of the Monarchy's coal and 84 percent of its lignite. Of the Austro-Hungarian industries, the figures were these: metallurgical products, 60 percent; chemicals, 75 percent; textiles, 75 percent; glass, 92 percent; porcelain, 100 percent; sugar refineries, 92 percent; breweries,

57 percent; leather, 70 percent; paper, 75 percent. One did not have to be a professional economist to know that the products of these industries could not be absorbed by the domestic market alone. Of all industrial goods, 50 to 60 percent had to be marketed abroad, and in some of the luxury industries, located mainly in the Sudetenland, the percentage often approached 100. The harsh fact of life was that Czechoslovak prosperity depended on international trade at prewar levels.

The outer ring of Secessionist States—Yugoslavia, Rumania, and Poland—had many of the same industrial problems. All three lacked the necessary capital to exploit their very considerable natural resources. Caught in the cross fire of World War I, they had been unable to participate in the industrial development which took place in most belligerent countries. Now they had to face the task of coordinating systems of transportation designed for different geographic units. Rail connections were almost nonexistent between the three partitioned sections of Poland, between Transylvania and the Regat, between Slovenia and Croatia, and between Croatia and Serbia.

Politicians and economists, especially during the 1930s, agonized over the duplication of industries in the Successor States and the decline of trade and prosperity. The solution seemed to lie in a return to the large trading area that had existed in the Danube region before the war. The Secessionist States would have nothing to do with a reconstruction of the Habsburg Monarchy which they feared would revive the financial supremacy of Vienna and Budapest. But the formation of a Danubian economic union including all the Successor States except Poland appeared feasible to many idealists, particularly those not living in the area. The fact of the matter was, however, that the economic ambitions of the Danube countries made such a union impossible. Hungary, Yugoslavia, and Rumania would have been interested in cooperating if they could have found satisfactory outlets for their agricultural surpluses. But the only food-importing countries—Austria and Czechoslovakia—were determined to make themselves self-sufficient, and they nearly succeeded. The same two countries, on the other hand, were anxious to find markets for their industrial exports, whereas the agrarian states made it their national policy to develop industries of their own. Outside powers like Italy and Germany were opposed to any economic federation in the Danube which might hamper their own exports into the region. Not even the Little Entente states of Czechoslovakia, Yugoslavia, and Rumania could work out mutually beneficial trade agreements other than for Czech munitions exports. Nor did they have much commerce with their Western ally, France.

The decline of international trade was a continuation of a trend well established by 1914 and rapidly accelerated by the war. We have seen how Hungary and the Austrian crownlands jealously hoarded their own resources during the war; when it ended, the new governments maintained controls over trade. And nationalism, which became an all-consuming obsession, above all in East Central Europe, compelled statesmen to subordinate real economic interests to national prestige and power.

The result was the levying of tariffs, which in 1931 were twice as high as those of 1913. Trade between Austria and Czechoslovakia in 1935 was one-sixth the volume of that existing between the two areas before the war. Largely because of this decline, per capita income in the Danube countries in 1937 was substantially lower than it had been in prewar years, despite vastly improved methods of production. Economic advancements were made in some fields, but usually at the expense of other aspects of a nation's economy. Austria, for example, increased its foodstuffs, but to the detriment of its industries. Yugoslavia, Rumania, and Hungary enlarged their industrial base, but with harmful effects to agricultural production. In short, East Central Europe was retrogressing in the 1930s. And the cause could not be attributed to the Depression alone.

Cultural Stagnation

The effects of this economic backsliding were nowhere more apparent than in cultural standards. Vienna, in particular, was devastated by the collapse of the Habsburg Monarchy and the bankruptcy of the Austrian Republic. The University of

Vienna, which had previously served an empire of 53 million, not to mention the Balkan states, now found itself in a country with one-seventh the Monarchy's population. Student enrollment declined from a prewar high of 10,000 to less than 6000. In the early postwar years state subsidies dwindled to a mere trickle. Professors earned the equivalent of 10 to 12 dollars a month, not enough to buy one suit of clothes a year. Few scholars could afford foreign books, and new equipment for scientific laboratories was a luxury beyond the means of the university for many years. Cultural institutions, not only in Austria and Hungary but to a lesser extent in the Secessionist States as well, were obliged to live off the intellectual and material capital accumulated over the centuries in the Habsburg Monarchy. Even today the visitor to the great museums in Vienna cannot help but notice the paucity of exhibits acquired after 1914.

Educational institutions assigned to alien governments by the peace treaties suffered the most tragic fate. The venerable University of Pressburg (Possony in Magyar, Bratislava in Slovak) was completely de-Magyarized by the Czechoslovak government, and its entire staff relocated in the new Hungary. In Yugoslavia virtually all primary and secondary Magyar schools were closed and their instructors forced to flee to Hungary.

The one bright spot in the otherwise dreary cultural panorama was the continued flourishing of music in Vienna, above all at the State Opera, where between 1919 and 1924 performances were directed by the dazzling baton of Richard Strauss. The Vienna Philharmonia Orchestra and the Society of the Friends of Music upheld the incomparable concert traditions of the city, and in Salzburg the annual summer festival attracted music lovers from all over the Western world.

The Nationality Question

Of the problems confronting the new national states after 1918 the nationality issue was undoubtedly the most vexing and ultimately the most disastrous. Presumably the issue had been settled, or nearly so, by the peace treaties. By any statistical count, more people lived in nation-states than before the war. Yet somehow the minority problem refused to go away.

The new minorities, although less numerous, were more urbanized, better educated, and more politically articulate than prewar minorities. The latter had included Ruthenes, Rumanians, Slovaks, and Serbs, all of them having comparatively low literacy rates and consisting mainly of peasants and small-town dwellers. Except for a handful of intellectuals, these people had no interest in politics. The same could hardly be said of the new minorities, who were primarily Germans and Magyars. Not only were they politically sophisticated, they also considered themselves culturally superior to their rustic Slavic neighbors. This superiority had been implicitly recognized by many members of the old minorities who had eagerly sought assimilation into the "master" nationalities. But after the war assimilation largely ceased. Slavs and some Jews who had earlier been assimilated into a majority group often retro-assimilated, but not the ethnic Germans or Magyars.

In 1914 an Austrian Slav, even though he did not live in a nation-state of his own, had not officially belonged to a minority. His political, social, economic, and cultural standards had been steadily on the rise since 1848 or earlier, and the outlook was encouraging for still further improvements. By contrast, the postwar minority member found himself in a nation-state whose real, if not official, policy was to denationalize and assimilate him and his people. There was little hope for any significant improvement in his condition so long as the international *status quo* remained unchanged. Prewar minorities had rarely favored the breakup of the Austro-Hungarian Monarchy; the new minorities longed for the complete destruction of the new order.

The new minorities were given safeguards which in 1919 seemed adequate for a satisfactory political and cultural life. The "minority treaties" mentioned earlier were intended to guarantee minorities the free use of their language in private life as well as public primary education in regions where they formed a substantial proportion of the population (usually 20 percent). Actually the treaties fell far short of what the Austrian nationalities had enjoyed in both theory and practice before 1914 and did not go beyond what the Hungarian minorities were granted on paper in 1868. As we have seen, they offered minorities no economic protection whatever. The treaties where respected, as in Austria, were enough to pacify small, inarticulate minorities having no political ambitions. But for larger nationalities that demanded real political power they had little value. More often than not the signatory powers violated them with impunity. Their significance, in fact, lay only in the bitterness they aroused toward the League of Nations on the part of both the minorities whose complaints brought few meaningful improvements, and the treaty states, whose dirty linen was being dragged into view.

Proportional representation and democracy were the other guarantors of fair minority treatment. Both practices turned into mirages. Proportional representation made some sense in a state like prewar Austria where no nationality had an absolute majority. Each ethnic group could sell its votes to whatever coalition offered the most concessions. In a unitary nation-state like Italy, however, where the South Tyrolese were outnumbered 160 to 1, or even in Czechoslovakia, where the Sudeten Germans were outvoted by the Czechs only 2 to 1, proportional representation was a smoke screen behind which minorities were powerless. In such a system the minorities could hardly be blamed for having little respect for what passed for democracy. Strong local autonomy was the one thing that could provide minorities with real assurance of political and cultural liberty. This had long been demanded by the smaller nationalities of the Habsburg Monarchy, yet it was the very thing that the new *Herrenvolk* dared not concede. A vicious circle was soon established. National minorities were denied regional autonomy because their loyalty was in doubt, and they remained disloyal because they were given no self-government.

The new minorities lived among people who, for the most part, lacked the linguistic skills or administrative experience to rule aliens with any degree of success. The Austrians, who were master linguists and had learned over the centuries the fine art of ruling other nationalities, were left by the Treaty of

St. Germain with next to no minorities. In one state there was a pitiful shortage of administrative talent, in the next a tragic surplus.

Czechoslovakia was the Successor State with far and away the most delicate nationality problem, comparable only to that of the Habsburg Monarchy. Austria-Hungary had had eleven nationalities; Czechoslovakia, with only one-quarter the population, had seven. Nor were those seven any more alike in their economic and cultural standards. The principle difference between the two states, however, lay not in their size or number of nationalities, but in their philosophy toward nationalism. The Austrian half of the Habsburg Monarchy had been a genuine multinational state both in theory and practice; Czechoslovakia in its philosophy and constitution was a nation-state. And this was at the heart of its nationality problem. Its national minorities were among the best treated in Europe. Yet it was not so much their treatment which rankled as their minority status. The Sudeten Germans thought that the Historic Provinces belonged as much to themselves (if not more so) as to the Czechs. If they had been granted complete equality in 1918, it is possible that they would have become as reconciled to the state as did the Swedish minority in Finland. But for the Czechs to have made the Germans equal partners was a political-philosophical impossibility. Having rebelled against the multinational Habsburg Monarchy in the sacred name of nationalism, the Czechs could not now set up a miniature multinational state of their own.

Denied real equality, the Sudeten Germans behaved in the Czech Parliament in the same obstructive manner as had the Czechs in the Austrian Reichsrat. After the German Republic signed the Locarno agreements in 1925 (which included a treaty of arbitration with Czechoslovakia), the more moderate Sudetens assumed that Germany had abandoned revisionism. So in 1926 members of the German Agrarian and Christian Social parties made their peace with the Czech state and joined the government, followed three years later by the German Social Democratic party. But their move represented no sincere change of heart. Like the prewar Czechs and Galician Poles, the Sudeten Germans were loyal to the establishment only when there was no alternative.

As for specific grievances, the Sudetens had little cause for complaint. The German University of Prague was unmolested (it was the only minority university in Europe after the war) and German-speaking people were proportionally represented in the teaching profession. After 1933 the German language press was freer by far than that of the Third Reich. It was true, though, that Czech language examinations for the civil service were made deliberately hard for German-speaking people. Sudeten Germans were also badly underrepresented in the central ministries in Prague, just as the Czechs had been in Vienna before the war. And when the Great Depression struck, the luxury industries of the Sudetenland were more severely affected than were the heavy industries of the Czech districts.

The Slovak problem was only slightly less dangerous to the Czechs. But Slovakia was primarily a domestic issue, whereas the Sudetenland was also an international one. The Czechs hurt their own cause by pretending that no Slovak problem existed. In their wartime propaganda and again at Paris Czech spokesmen consistently spoke of a "Czechoslovak" nationality and language. Actually there were two peoples and two languages which remained distinct throughout the entire history of the First Republic. The Slovaks, in fact, were more conscious of their separate identity in 1938 than in 1918.

Real friction between the two peoples began already with the Czech occupation of the Slovak districts of Hungary in December 1918. Magyar officials were immediately dismissed from their posts; but with only 750 to 1000 educated and nationally conscious Slovaks to choose from, most of the vacant bureaucratic positions had to be filled by Czechs. The Slovaks' need for Czech assistance only increased their resentment at having their homeland invaded by over 100,000 Czech officials. With the rise of Slovak educational standards, however, this sore spot was gradually healed as Slovaks were able to replace retiring Czechs.

But economic problems were far more enduring. Without the prewar subsidies of the Hungarian government the industries of Slovakia were unable to compete with the more advanced ones in the Historic Provinces. Over a third of the Slovak enterprises had to be liquidated shortly after the war. The rivers of this area, all flowing into the Hungarian plain, had been used to float logs downstream to Hungarian buyers. The Czechs, having more timber than they themselves needed, could not replace the lost markets.

All the political and economic difficulties of Slovakia were also found in Ruthenia, only in a far more intensified form. Living at the very tip of the Czechoslovak tail, the Ruthenes were closer to the capitals of Hungary, Austria, Yugoslavia, Rumania, Bulgaria, and Poland than they were to Prague. Transportation costs to the population centers of western Czechoslovakia were so high that fully 70 percent of the Ruthene industries disappeared after 1918. Peasants fared no better. In the autumn of 1919 simple agricultural workers making their annual pilgrimage to the Hungarian wheat harvest had to be informed by Czech authorities that this was now impossible, since they had been "liberated" the year before.

Like a British colony, or prewar Bosnia-Herzegovina, the region was well administered by the Czechs. But like most colonial people, the Ruthenes wanted not so much good government as their own government. The promised autonomy, however, did not materialize until 1938. Expensive to govern, impossible to defend, it is hard to see what the Czechs gained from this remote corner of Europe. For the Ruthenes, liberation meant grinding poverty worse than anything they had known in Hungary.

The nationality question in Yugoslavia was confined in large measure to the relationship between the three majority peoples. The official national minorities, numbering 2.5 million out of a total population of 12 million, were scattered along the fringes of the country and presented no great threat to the state. They were suppressed by the Serbs with a ruthlessness unknown in any other country except Italy, and later Nazi Germany.

The real nationality issue in the South Slav state was the lack of a common denominator between the majority peoples. The "Yugoslav" idea had been confined, as we have seen, almost exclusively to the Croats before and during the war; it vanished into thin air as soon as the Serbo-Croat merger took place. The differences in historical development, religion, and even alphabets were more important than any abstract ethnic identity. The Slovenes and Croats were Catholics and Central Europeans who looked to Rome, Vienna, or Budapest for cultural inspiration. The Greek Orthodox Serbs had lived under the shadow of the Ottoman Turks for over four centuries and were regarded by former Austro-Hungarian subjects as "Orientals."

The Slovenes' disaffection was tempered by near administrative autonomy as well as by their need for Serbian military support against Italy. Even the violently anti-Serb Croats hesitated to break away from Yugoslavia completely lest they be partitioned by Italy and Hungary. When King Alexander, at wit's end over the Serbo-Croat feud, proposed a voluntary separation in 1928, moderate Croats turned the offer down. The radical Croat Peasant party, however, was not above conspiring against Belgrade with the representatives of the Italian and Hungarian foreign ministries.

The Serbo-Croatian cold war persisted under the royal dictatorship during the 1930s until finally, on the eve of the Second World War, an autonomous Croatian state was created. The arrangement bore a striking resemblance to the Croat-Hungarian *Nagodba,* or Compromise, of 1868, as the Croatians were conceded their own diet and governor. But foreign affairs, defense, commerce, transportation, and public security still rested with Belgrade authorities. The settlement was generous, but neither the Croats nor the Serbs were fully satisfied. Radical Croats insisted that they had more liberty under Hungary. Twenty years of history had only proved that it was easier to create a Yugoslav state than a Yugoslav people.

Rumania was the Successor State least troubled by nationality problems. The Transylvanian Rumanians, unlike the Croats or Slovaks, never developed a separatist movement, and the minorities were too jealous of each other to form a common front. The Rumanians made doubly sure of this by giving preferential treatment to the Germans. Numbering over 700,000 the Germans received more cultural privileges than they had been given by the Magyars before the war. They soon lost interest in returning to Hungary. The Rumanians also benefited politically (but certainly not economically) from their high birth rate and migration to the cities. Whereas in 1910 they had made up only 19.6 percent of the urban population of Transylvania compared to 62 percent for the Magyars, the comparable figures in 1930 were 35.3 percent for the Rumanians and 38.4 percent for the Magyars. The Rumanians were slowly solidifying their grip on their new western territories, although the Magyars remained strong in extreme western and northern Transylvania.

The plight of Polish minorities was scandalous. Having next to no representation in Parliament, they were also subjected to intense Polonization. About a million Germans in the Corridor found life in Poland so intolerable that they moved to Germany. For those who stayed behind, Nazism was too attractive to resist. The Germans in Poland, however, were well off compared to the Ukrainians. Cultural and political rights won by the Habsburg Ukrainians were largely lost after 1918, and the autonomy promised in 1923 was never actuated. The minority problem did unify the Poles of Austrian, Prussian, and Russian background; but exasperation at German representations in the League over alleged violations of the minority treaty led the Poles to denounce their treaty in 1934, an action which met stern international censure. It was a daring step for a state which needed all the foreign support it could get.

International Affairs

Poland's go-it-alone philosophy toward its minority treaty was indicative of a state of mind which, while particularly evident among Poles, was also typical of other Successor States. The postwar impotence of Germany and the Soviet Union gave all the countries of East Central Europe a dangerous illusion of security. International cooperation, except for certain limited objectives, seemed a superfluous luxury.

This divisiveness was not always understood in the West. Many a Frenchman was convinced that Czechoslovakia and Poland, for example, were genuine substitutes for the prewar Russian alliance. The two Slavic states were indeed prepared to join forces with France against possible German aggression. France and Poland concluded an alliance in 1921, and four years later Czechoslovakia adhered to the French security system. But Prague refused to sign any military convention, fearing that the Germans would interpret such an action as a new "encirclement." And even Paris hesitated to make the tie with Warsaw too close, because Poland, with its long and exposed border with Germany could be a military liability. Already in 1925 relations between France and its eastern allies cooled perceptively when the Locarno Pact revealed France's greater interest in its Rhine frontier than in the permanency of Germany's eastern boundaries. Czechs and Poles were well-nigh excluded from the Swiss meeting, a treatment foreshadowing Czechoslovakia's status at the Munich conference thirteen years later.

Pilsudski's return to power in 1926 further splintered the anti-German front. The Polish dictator typified many of his countrymen in holding strong Czechophobe views. The Poles, with their ancient agrarian and aristocratic traditions, regarded the bourgeois Czechs as cold and calculating. By contrast, the Poles had kindly feelings toward the Hungarians (which were reciprocated), whose way of life resembled their own. Small wonder then that Poland was unsympathetic with Czechoslovakia's (and the Little Entente's) goal of stifling Hungarian revisionism.

Czech and Polish policies clashed even more conspicuously vis-à-vis the Soviet Union. Prewar and wartime Pan-Slavism lingered on in Czechoslovakia after the war. Russia, with whom the Czechs had no common frontier and no territorial disputes, could safely be seen as a potential ally against Germany. Poland's contact with the Russians had been much more intimate, but less congenial. The brutal suppression of periodic Polish revolts in the nineteenth century was not forgotten. Nor was the near conquest of Warsaw by the Bolsheviks in 1920. And the Czechs' use of the Russian invasion as an opportunity to occupy Teschen was something few Poles could forgive. Understandably, any move on the part of Czechoslovakia (or France) to improve relations with the Soviets met with deep Polish misgivings. Pilsudski hoped to have good relations with both Russians and Germans. But for him, unlike the Czechs, an alliance with the Soviet Union was out of the question, since Poland would inevitably be the weaker partner. He was convinced that Russia had not abandoned its traditional imperialism.

Poland has often been chastised for not joining the Little Entente in order to form a solid bloc of *status quo* powers stretching from the Baltic to the Adriatic. Polish foreign policy in the interwar period is subject to criticism on a variety of grounds, but the failure to join the Little Entente is understandable at the very least: The Little Entente did not address itself to Poland's basic fear—Russian and German revisionism; instead, it was directed against a restoration of the Habsburgs and a modification of Hungary's frontiers, neither of which interested the Poles.

Winston Churchill, among other Western observers, was captivated by what appeared on paper to be the great power status of the Little Entente. In a speech to the House of Commons delivered in 1938 he optimistically claimed that

> taken singly, the three countries of the Little Entente may be called powers of the second rank, but they are very powerful and vigorous states and united they are a Great Power. They have hitherto been and are still, united by the closest military agreement. Together they make the complement of a Great Power and of the military machinery of a Great Power. Rumania has the oil, Yugoslavia has the minerals and raw materials. Both have large armies, both are mainly supplied with munitions from Czechoslovakia.[2]

Churchill's assessment was wildly exaggerated. Except for the number of men under arms, the Little Entente had none of the attributes of a major power. Its only common objectives were of small concern to the outside world. On the big issues no agreement could be reached. Czechoslovakia wanted support against Germany, but this did not interest Rumania and Yugoslavia. Rumania was worried about the Soviet Union, but Czechoslovakia and Yugoslavia were either pro-Russian or neutral. Yugoslavia's relations with Italy were nearly always at the breaking point, but its two partners had perfectly correct dealings

---

[2] *The Second World War, The Gathering Storm* (New York: Bantam Books, 1961), p. 244.

with the Fascists. The Little Entente consistently provided France with three votes in the League of Nations, but was useless collectively as an anti-German military combination.

In truth, the Little Entente was nothing more than the product of a refurbished Compromise of 1867: a bargain among the new *Herrenvolk* to keep the old ruling nationalities severely in their place. Fervent supporters of boundary changes in 1918, the Little Entente now regarded international frontiers as sacrosanct and branded revisionist countries as "aggressors."

Old Myths and New Realities

By the time Adolf Hitler came to power in 1933 the assumptions of the Paris Peace Conference had dissolved into mythology. The Slovaks had not become Czechoslovaks; the Slovenes and Croats had refused to turn into Yugoslavs; the German Austrians were still more German than Austrian. Peaceful territorial revision envisaged in Article XIX of the League of Nations charter was repeatedly blocked by the *status quo* powers, above all, by the Little Entente and France. Democracy in most of the Successor States had been incapable of winning a popular consensus, but the dictatorships which replaced it had even less mass support. The countries of East Central Europe were splintered both domestically and internationally. Chances of their forming an "insurmountable barrier" to great power imperialism were hardly favorable.

CHAPTER FIVE

Hitler's First Conquests

Austria and the Anschluss *Question*

The weakest link in the chain of states surrounding Germany was the Republic of Austria. By no stretch of the imagination could it be considered part of the "insurmountable barrier" to German expansion. On the contrary, many Austrians continued to favor union with Germany throughout the entire interwar period. *Anschluss* agitation abated after the Allied veto at Paris, but even during the relatively prosperous years between 1925 and 1929 numerous demonstrations in favor of union took place. All three political parties in Austria made *Anschluss* part of their program until 1933. In foreign affairs *Anschluss* was the only bargaining weapon the Austrian government possessed, as it served to blackmail the Allies into granting Austria much needed loans.

With the coming of the Great Depression *Anschluss* sentiments in Austria inevitably quickened. The Republic's economy had never been sound; even in the so-called good year of 1929 industrial production was only 95 percent of the prewar level for the same area, and 17 percent of the country's workers holding unemployment insurance were out of work. With its extreme dependence on foreign trade Austria was harder hit by the depression than other industrialized states.

To imagine that union with Germany, itself impoverished, would cure Austria's economy was naive. At best a merger could have brought only political or psychological benefits. These were exactly the aims, however, inspiring secret negotiations in 1930 for a customs union between the two German-speaking countries. The project was suddenly announced to a startled world on March 21, 1931. International reaction was predictable; Great Britain and the United States were sympathetic, but the *status quo* powers, France and the Little Entente, saw the plan as a disguised *Anschluss*. France, still relatively unaffected by the Depression, had the financial muscle to make its objections stick. Its price for a loan desperately needed by Austria was the scrapping of the customs union. Austria complied; France had won a great diplomatic victory—its last. The German and Austrian governments were humiliated, and democracy in both countries suffered another slap in the face; the Nazi cause was given a shot in the arm.

Equally damaging to Austrian democracy was the cabinet crisis of May 1932. Engelbert Dollfuss, unable to secure the support of either the Pan-German party or the Social Democrats for the formation of a new cabinet, was forced to turn to the fascist *Heimwehr*. It is difficult to see what alternative he had under the circumstances. Yet his decision had fatal consequences for democracy. The clerical-legitimist wing of the *Heimwehr* was receiving financial and military assistance from Benito Mussolini, who used the Chancellor's dependence on *Heimwehr* support to push him toward authoritarian rule. Dollfuss had inclinations in this direction anyway, as a representative of the "front generation" which had reached maturity during the world war. Its members had learned to associate democracy with military defeat (since both came to Austria at the same

(From left to right) Engelbert Dollfuss, chancellor of Austria; Gyula von Gömbös, prime minister of Hungary; General Karl Vaugoin, Austrian minister of war; and Major Emil Fey, Austrian security minister, at a meeting in Vienna in 1933. *(National Archives)*

time), and parliamentarianism with frustrating ideological conflict and obstructionism. Military efficiency seemed applicable to political problems, particularly during crises. In Italy, Germany, Hungary, Poland, Yugoslavia, and Rumania men of this persuasion infused politics with militancy and fanaticism.

In March 1933 Dollfuss allowed Parliament to "dissolve itself" on a ridiculous technicality involving voting procedures. The Chancellor thus became a dictator if perhaps the mildest one in Europe. A smattering of anti-Semitism, an espousal of the leadership principle, a denunciation of Marxism, a denial of civil liberties, and even the establishment of concentration camps became identified with the regime. But racism was certainly not extreme, internationalism was placed above nationalism, ties with the Roman Catholic Church were strengthened, imperialism was rejected, traditional Austrian values were revived, and there was scarcely a hint of terrorism. Except for trappings, the basic tone of life changed little. In short, the regime was authoritarian, not totalitarian. The very mildness of the regime, however, may have been its undoing. By disdaining the emotionalism of Nazism and Italian Fascism the Austrian dictatorship never acquired a mass following. The "Fatherland Front," which Dollfuss founded in 1934 after the elimination of all political parties, failed to attract a clientele beyond the Chancellor's own Christian Social party. The Austrian dictatorship, in fact, satisfied almost no one. For the genuine democrat, it was anathema; for the totalitarian, a pale imitation of the German and Italian models. As a means of taking the wind out of Nazi sails it was a complete failure.

Dollfuss lacked the charisma of a Hitler or a Mussolini. His tiny stature (he was less than five feet tall) and peasant drawl rendered him ludicrous in the eyes of his enemies, who sarcastically labeled him "Millimetternich." Catholics and especially peasants were attracted to his simple, cordial manners, and the West romanticized him as a David battling heroically against the Nazi Goliath; but none of this could be added up to fanatical support.

From the moment he took office Dollfuss was subjected to pressures from every side. The *Heimwehr* and its Italian sponsor pushed for the elimination of Social Democracy; the Austrian and German Nazis strove for *Gleichschaltung* (coordination) of Austria into the status of another *Gau,* or district, of the Nazi party. The weakest pressure came from the West. Although frowning on the increasingly antidemocratic character of the Dollfuss regime, the West was ill-disposed toward "interfering in the internal affairs of another country," especially if that country was pursuing an anti-Nazi course. In practice, this meant that the West was giving Italy a free hand, a hegemony it exercised until 1936 when the Italians "gallantly" stepped aside in favor of Nazi Germany.

Until then the nominal independence of Austria was considered vital to Italian security. Hitler's professions in *Mein Kampf* notwithstanding, the Duce was never able to convince himself that German expansion would halt at the Brenner. An *Anschluss* would jeopardize not only Italy's grip on the South Tyrol but also its grandiose plans for annexing the Dalmatian coast of Yugoslavia and dominating the Danube Valley. Italy already had a revisionist friend in Hungary; Yugoslavia could be nearly surrounded if Austria were brought into the Italian orbit.

One thing stood in Mussolini's path: Austrian Social Democracy. If Dollfuss were forced to eliminate the Socialists, the Western powers would be offended and the Chancellor would be securely in Mussolini's pocket. Naturally, the Duce disguised his motives with chatter about the need to deprive the Austrian Nazis of their anti-Marxist weapon, but Dollfuss was too intelligent to be taken in. His negotiations with the Austrian Nazis in the winter of 1933–1934 clearly represent a determined effort to escape the tutelage of the Italian dictator and his *Heimwehr* protégés. But the Nazis would settle for nothing short of lordship over the Austrian house. Finally, in February 1934 the *Heimwehr* took matters into its own hands by expelling Socialists from a number of provincial governments; the object was to forestall a possible Dollfuss–Social Democratic party (SDP) reconciliation. Almost simultaneously local Socialist headquarters in Linz were searched by police. When a handful of left-wing Socialists tried to retaliate, a brief civil war ensued. In three

A demonstration by young Nazis in Vienna. The poster reads: "Stamp out the Jewish press! Lies, corruption, trash!" *(National Archives)*

days of fighting, 289 people were killed, about 700 wounded, and another 4000 arrested.

As civil wars go, this affair was tame enough; but it resulted in the outlawing of the Social Democratic party and all its affiliates. The tiny Communist movement gained some new converts, but most Social Democrats simply became politically passive. A few felt that if they had to live under a dictatorship it might as well be provided by the efficient, prosperous, anticlerical German Nazis.

The international repercussions of the fighting served to isolate Austria diplomatically. Britain, France, and Czechoslovakia reacted with pious horror, although they did nothing to compel Dollfuss to restore democracy or the Socialist party.

The German Policy of Peaceful Penetration in Austria: The First Phase

The civil war so undermined the popularity of the Dollfuss regime that Nazis in both Austria and Germany were convinced that victory was imminent. Overt German interference in Austrian affairs was unnecessary and certainly undesirable from the diplomatic point of view, since it would alarm the Western democracies. This had to be avoided while Nazi Germany was still defenseless. Such was the reasoning behind the policy of "peaceful penetration" Germany pursued off and on from 1933 to the beginning of 1938. An out-and-out *Anschluss* was definitely not a part of these plans, as nothing would have been more likely to provoke the West. Annexation of Austria would have been superfluous, however, if the country had already been Nazified and its economy and foreign policy coordinated with those of the Third Reich.

When the German Nazis came to power in January 1933 the chances for a repetition in Austria seemed excellent. The last free elections held in April 1932 had given the National Socialist German Workers' party (NSDAP) of Austria three times as many votes in three provinces as it had received in all nine provinces two years before. Actually the victory, although certainly impressive, was not indicative of an approaching Nazi landslide. Nazi gains had come principally at the expense of the Pan-German People's party, while the Christian Social and the Social Democratic parties, which unlike the Pan-German People's party had well developed ideologies, held their own. Since the clericals and Socialists were relatively stronger than their German counterparts, it is unlikely that the Austrian Nazis ever could have won more than 30 to 35 percent of the national vote in a free election.

As early as May 1933 it was becoming apparent to Nazi leaders that the Austrian government was not going to oblige them by collapsing of its own accord. Chancellor Dollfuss used his newly acquired dictatorial powers to fight the Nazis by outlawing first their uniforms and insignia, then in June, after a series of Nazi outrages, the party itself. Even before this last move Hitler reacted with an economic boycott (including a prohibition of tourist traffic to Austria) and a massive propaganda offensive. When the Austrian NSDAP was declared illegal, a new *Landesleitung* (State Directorate) was established in Munich under the authority of the Reich party leadership *(Reichsparteileitung)*. This step could hardly be reconciled with the original policy of nonintervention.

Accelerated propaganda and economic attacks on Austria only antagonized the Western Powers, the very thing the German Foreign Office was trying to avoid. In a memorandum dated August 28, 1933, the British Foreign Secretary, Sir Robert Vansittart, noted that Austria was "the first of a series of challenges. . . . If Hitler wins this first round he will be hard to hold."[1] Unfortunately, not all British statesmen, either in 1933 or later, were so perceptive.

Continued Nazi provocations led to a joint communique issued on February 17, 1934, by the governments of Britain, France, and Italy reaffirming their interest in Austrian independence. A month later the "Rome Protocols" were signed in which Italy, Austria, and Hungary agreed to bilateral trade agreements

---

[1] *Memorandum by Sir Vansittart on "The Present and Future position in Europe," Documents on British Foreign Policy,* Second Series, V, p. 552.

and consultations to coordinate their foreign policies. In effect, Rome had established a protectorate over the two Danube states.

Hitler now had to reconsider his Austrian policy. What he envisaged was a return to genuine peaceful penetration emphasizing propaganda glorifying achievements of National Socialism in Germany. At the same time the illegal party in Austria would be expanded. Once tranquillity had been restored the Nazis would work toward regaining legality for the party, freedom for the Nazi press, the release of Nazi political prisoners, and the appointment of Nazis to important posts in the Dollfuss cabinet. Then subversion could begin again in earnest.

When propaganda, terror, and even negotiations failed, Theo Habicht, the head of the *Landesleitung*, began to contemplate more forceful alternatives. He complained to the German foreign minister, Konstantin von Neurath, "that the total ban on propaganda against the Austrian government, as well as the instruction issued to him personally not to make any more speeches of any kind against Austria, could result in the gradual disintegration of the National Socialist movement in Austria."[2]

Such considerations probably convinced Habicht of the need for a *Putsch* against the Dollfuss regime. On June 6, 1934, he told Hitler that the Austrian army was plotting to compel the government to accept an *Anschluss*. Hitler agreed that under these circumstances the party in both Austria and Germany could offer open support. But Habicht was either lying or grossly overoptimistic. The *Putsch*, which began in Vienna on July 25, 1934, was actually the work of a Nazi SS unit supported in the provinces (principally Styria and Carinthia) by the Pan-German wing of the *Heimwehr* which had seceded from the parent organization and formed a fighting alliance *(Kampfgemeinschaft)* with the Nazis in 1933. The Austrian army, far from joining the *Putsch*, helped to crush it. Hitler's gullibility is astonishing. Eleven years earlier similar wishful thinking about the German army had led to the failure of his own Beer Hall *Putsch* in Munich.

[2] *Memorandum by the Director of Department II*, March 16, 1934, *Documents on German Foreign Policy*, Series C, II, pp. 616–617.

The Austrian *Putsch* was poorly planned and even more poorly executed. Some members of the federal cabinet escaped capture, and the conspirators appeared bloodthirsty when Dollfuss was shot (perhaps accidentally) and allowed to bleed to death without the aid of a physician or priest. The Austrian public remained almost completely passive or else supported the government. Not even all the Nazi SA and SS units carried out their assigned roles. The minister of education, Kurt von Schuschnigg, was able to form a new cabinet and the Putschists in the chancellery were soon forced to surrender.

The *Putsch* created an international sensation. Mussolini, furious at the death of his friend and protégé, ostentatiously activated 100,000 troops already on the Brenner. The West saw in the *Putsch* a fresh example of Nazi barbarism, coming as it did only four weeks after "the night of the long knives" when numerous Germans had been unceremoniously murdered. For the Führer himself, the *Putsch* was probably the low mark in his prewar diplomacy. Nazi Germany was isolated.

Peaceful Penetration Renewed

Peaceful penetration and the July *Putsch* both failed because there had been no centralized control over Germany's Austrian policy. Hitler, the Foreign Ministry, the *Landesleitung,* and the illegal Austrian Nazi party all had a voice, but no group or individual exercised decisive influence. In desperation Hitler turned to a man who had the determination — some would call it cunning — to centralize Germany's Austrian policy in his own hands and return to the original policy of peaceful penetration. Hitler now agreed to legality in foreign affairs, just as he had done in domestic affairs after his beer-hall disaster.

Franz von Papen was Hitler's choice as the new German envoy to Vienna. A former chancellor, von Papen's reputation had been badly tarnished in the West by his machinations leading to Hitler's appointment as chancellor in January 1933. But he had redeemed himself to some extent by a courageous speech delivered at the University of Marburg on June 17, 1934, attacking Nazi excesses. As a practicing Catholic, a conservative, and a monarchist, von Papen could gain easy access to influential Austrian political circles.

Before accepting Hitler's appointment von Papen laid down a number of conditions. Habicht had to go and the *Landes-leitung* in Munich had to be dissolved; all relations between the German and Austrian Nazi parties were to be severed, and the *Anschluss* was to be consummated only by strictly evolutionary means, not by the use of force. The fulfillment of these conditions would relax international tensions until Austria was forgotten. Internal disputes in Austria would reappear as the external danger receded. There was nothing new about this policy—except its centralization in the hands of a single man.

Von Papen was aided in his effort to subvert the Austrian government by several aspects of the new Chancellor's character. In many respects Schuschnigg was like his predecessor. He and Dollfuss were fervent Catholics, disciples of Ignaz Seipel, sincere Austrian patriots, and anti-Nazis. Unfortunately, they also shared some less admirable traits—skepticism of democracy and hostility toward Socialism. There were also important differences. Schuschnigg, a highly polished, impeccably educated aristocrat, lacked the personal magnetism and the common touch of Dollfuss, the son of a peasant. His dignity, reserve, and natural shyness made Schuschnigg appear cold and disdainful at a time when charisma was in vogue throughout the Continent. The Austrian government under Schuschnigg became an old-fashioned autocracy, mild, decent, but uninspiring. It was not a state for which, and Schuschnigg not a man for whom, Austrians would gladly die.

A fatal weakness in Schuschnigg's political philosophy was his Pan-Germanism. It had little in common with the Nazi brand, of course, being largely cultural and historical. The Austrian people he regarded as simply one branch of the German "race." The Chancellor was not so much wrong as politically maladroit in emphasizing a philosophy that could hardly strengthen Austria's resolve to resist the *Anschluss*. Above all, his Pan-Germanism made an overtly anti-German policy impossible. Appeasement was the only alternative.

For more than a year following the July *Putsch,* Austria's

Kurt von Schuschnigg, chancellor of Austria, and Prince Rudiger von Starhemberg, leader of the Austrian *Heimwehr*, honor the victims of the July *Putsch*, August 3, 1934. *(National Archives)*

international position remained strong and appeasement was unnecessary. Vienna was uninterested in a *modus vivendi,* while tensions between the two countries aided the Austrian government at home and abroad. Austria's position was strengthened by an Italian-French consultative pact (January 1935) and still more by the April 1935 Stresa Conference at which Britain joined the two Latin states in reaffirming its support of Austrian independence.

Three-power unity in halting Nazi expansion, however, was more impressive on paper than in practice. The Stresa Conference chose to ignore the recent announcement of German rearmament which was a clear violation of the Versailles Treaty. A month later the British sanctioned the treaty breach by concluding a Naval Agreement with Berlin. This bilateral pact was a radical departure from the concept of collective security long advocated by the British. France, Italy, and Russia were offended at not having been consulted. When Mussolini began his invasion of Ethiopia in October 1935, many Frenchmen felt that since Britain had already betrayed League principles, there was no reason to oppose Italy's imperial ambitions.

The Ethiopian War was the turning point in Austria's struggle for survival. Britain backed the League against Italian aggression. France, forced to choose between Italy and Britain, chose Britain. Italy, forced to choose between its imperial designs in the Danube basin and the conquest of Ethiopia, opted for Ethiopia. Austria, forced to choose between the League and the West on the one hand and Italy on the other, reluctantly favored the latter. Before the end of 1935 the Stresa Front was dead and Austria was without an effective protector. Downing Street and the Quai d'Orsay showed a certain sympathy for Austria's dilemma, but the country's popularity sank among the British and French public.

Contributing still more to the shifting balance of power was the German remilitarization of the Rhineland in March 1936. The British historian A. J. P. Taylor has correctly pointed out the military insignificance of this move, since the French had long since abandoned an offensive strategy. Nevertheless, the psychological and diplomatic repercussions of the event were traumatic for Austria. The timid Franco-British response to the German action was taken by Vienna as conclusive proof of Western indifference to European affairs east of the Rhine. There now seemed to be no alternative to a compromise with the Third Reich.

So in July 1936 an agreement was reached with the German government. To the general public it looked like a victory for Schuschnigg. He had won formal German recognition of Austria's independence and a promise that Austrian Nazis would be given no aid or direction by Germany. The third clause about Austria being a "German State" was open to criticism, but the Austrian Chancellor had no intention of concluding an anti-German alliance in any case.

The dangerous part of the Austro-German understanding was a secret supplement known as the "Gentlemen's Agreement." Here it was agreed that press and cultural relations as well as trade and tourist traffic were to be restored; Austrian political prisoners were to be released; and two members of the "National Opposition" (pro-Nazis) were to be included in the Schuschnigg cabinet. In other words, Nazi propaganda activity in Austria could resume, although direct attacks on the government were precluded.

By far the most serious domestic effect of the Agreement was the growth of lethargy and political indifference among government supporters. Speeches even vaguely anti-Nazi could be condemned by National Socialists as violations of the "German State" clause, likewise the prosecution of Nazis in Austrian courts. Thus, peaceful penetration could go into high gear.

Chancellor Schuschnigg was under no illusions that the pact was without dangers or that Hitler would indefinitely respect Austria's independence. He gambled that it would improve Austria's economy and give the country a breathing spell during which the European balance of power might become more favorable. It never did.

The July Agreement was a great diplomatic victory for Hitler. Mussolini now implicitly recognized Austria as a German, not Italian, sphere of influence. He raised no objections when Schuschnigg eliminated the *Heimwehr* leader, Prince

Ernst Rüdiger von Starhemberg from the cabinet in October 1936 and later disbanded the *Heimwehr* itself. The latter move strengthened Schuschnigg's position within the government, but weakened his already shaky popular support. Mussolini's involvement in the Spanish Civil War, which began only six days after the signing of the July Agreement, cemented Italo-German friendship and made a restoration of Italian influence in Austria impossible.

The Czechs and French were suspicious of the Agreement but made no protests. Americans and Englishmen enthusiastically endorsed it. Typical of Anglo-American reaction was an editorial from a British periodical:

> There is no reason for Great Britain not to welcome this agreement. Even if Herr Hitler's calculation is that the closer embrace of the "two German states" must ultimately lead to the absorption of the weaker by the stronger, and even if one suspects that this calculation will justify itself, there is no reason to alter this verdict. The seizure of Austria by force would have provoked deep-seated hostility in this country. . . . But no such objection can be felt to the peaceful and gradual assimilation of Austria by Germany. . . . Public opinion in this country has never been altogether happy about the treaty prohibition on the union between the two countries. . . .[3]

This was also the view of the British government right through the *Anschluss*.

The Anschluss *and Its Consequences*

The noose around Austria's neck was tightened still further by Germany's economic penetration of east central and southeastern Europe. The policy did not originate with the Nazis. Gustav Stresemann, perennial foreign minister of the German Republic, had tried to make the same area a German sphere of economic interest; even imperial Germany had extensive commerce with the region. Hitler's innovation was tying economic

[3] "Dictator's Bargain" (editorial), *Spectator,* CLVII (July, 1936), p. 84.

penetration to his plans for political domination of the Continent.

The breakup of the Habsburg Monarchy, together with the Great Depression, played into the hands of the German dictator. Germany was the one major country willing to absorb agricultural surpluses. France was unable, Great Britain uninterested. Germany could pay high prices for food from the Danube basin by exporting its own manufactured products. The economies of Germany and the Successor States were therefore complementary. Nothing was especially covert about German economic policies. The Third Reich's new trading partners realized the political implications of increased commerce, but profited from the exchange and welcomed it.

Yugoslavia and Rumania, the most agrarian of the Successor States and the most remote from Germany geographically, had little fear of an *Anschluss*. For Rumania it meant more trade with Germany; for Yugoslavia it would also end once and for all the possibility of a Habsburg restoration which could attract Slovenes and Croats. A common border with Germany, moreover, might help to restrain Italy's ambitions in the Adriatic. For Hungary the *Anschluss* meant a likely increase in the sale of wheat. Czechoslovakia dissented. Although fearful of a Habsburg return, its economy competed with Germany's, and the Czechs did not enjoy the luxury of distance from the Nazi Behemoth. Beneš, however, although opposed to the *Anschluss*, did not actively resist Germany's strangulation of Austria. The Little Entente was therefore useless as an obstacle to the *Anschluss*, although all three member states had opposed it in 1919. Poland was simply indifferent to the issue, considering Austria remote from its interests. Ideology, moreover, provided the Secessionist States with no great rallying cry against Nazi Germany, since all of them, except Czechoslovakia, were dictatorships in the thirties. On the contrary, the Nazis' anti-Semitism was in high favor in at least Poland and Rumania.

The Western powers were also divided over the *Anschluss* question. France still favored Austrian independence, but its defensive military strategy and mentality impeded effective assistance. The British, particularly the Conservative party under Stanley Baldwin and Neville Chamberlain, simply did not want to get involved in what looked like a faraway fratricidal conflict between two branches of the German nation. Britons had been unenthusiastic about the prohibition of the *Anschluss* in 1918–1919; they were even more indifferent in the thirties. The general policy of the Foreign Office since the Peace Conference had been conciliation. Germany was seen as having legitimate grievances against Versailles. If these grievances could be appeased (the word did not yet have its present evil connotations), the causes of war would be removed. This line of reasoning made considerable sense when Germany's destiny was guided by a moderate statesman like Stresemann; it was sheer folly once the Nazis were in power.

The British leaders made no distinction in their policy between German democrats on the one hand and German racists and imperialists on the other. A guarantee of Austrian independence in 1937 would irritate Berlin. In November Prime Minister Chamberlain sent Lord Halifax, who shortly thereafter became foreign secretary, to visit Hitler at his mountain retreat near Berchtesgaden. Halifax cheerfully suggested to the Führer that changes in the European *status quo* were possible in Austria, Czechoslovakia, and Danzig. England was only "interested to see that any alterations should come through the course of peaceful evolution and that methods should be avoided which might cause far-reaching disturbances. . . ."[4] These words must have been music to the Reich Chancellor's ears since in the case of Austria, at least, no forceful seizure was even contemplated.

It was about the time of the Hitler-Halifax meeting that Hitler probably decided to speed up the "evolutionary" Austrian policy. An outright annexation was still not planned, but increased German military strength plus the obvious weakness and timidity of the West doubtless convinced him that his earlier caution was now unnecessary.

The actual events leading to the *Anschluss*, however, caught Hitler by surprise. Schuschnigg, not Hitler, took the

[4] Quoted in Keith Eubank, *Munich* (Norman, Okla.: University of Oklahoma Press, 1963), p. 19.

initiative. Everything both military and diplomatic had to be improvised by the German dictator in a couple of days. The drama began with the famous confrontation between Hitler and Schuschnigg at Berchtesgaden in mid-February 1938. The Führer, working himself into a rage, accused the Austrian Chancellor of violating the Gentlemen's Agreement. Surrounded by senior German generals he demanded that an Austrian pro-Nazi, Artur Seyss-Inquart, be given the crucial post of minister of interior, which would put him in charge of police. After a day of browbeating, Schuschnigg consented.

Convinced that Austria's *Gleichschaltung* was imminent, Schuschnigg made a desperate gamble: he called for a plebiscite to explode the Nazi myth of overwhelming Austrian support for the *Anschluss.* Here was a challenge Hitler could not ignore; he had to act or be humiliated.

Unfortunately, Schuschnigg gave the Führer ample reason to act. The plebiscite was a sham. The Austrian people were given no clear-cut choice between voting for or against the *Anschluss,* but only on the question: "For a free and German, Independent and social, Christian and united Austria; for freedom and work, and for the equality of all who declare for race and fatherland."[5] Even the Nazis were confused as to which way they should vote. Worse yet, the voting age was deliberately raised to twenty-four to exclude young Nazis, and only *"ja"* ballots were to be furnished. These arrangements betrayed the same lack of confidence in Austrian patriotism as military officials had shown in non-German speaking districts during the First World War.

Only when Hitler learned of the plebiscite did he decide on an invasion, and only when the invasion went unopposed by both Austria and the great powers did he decide on an undisguised *Anschluss.* In making this choice the German dictator showed no more respect for Austrian Nazis than he did for Schuschnigg. Seyss-Inquart and his colleagues wanted a National Socialist Austria, but a formally independent Austria

[5] Quoted in Gordon Shepherd, *The Austrian Odyssey* (London: Macmillan, 1957), p. 128.

Hitler and his entourage leaving Vienna after the *Anschluss*, March 1939. *(National Archives)*

nonetheless. Their exclusion from power after only twenty-four hours was a clue to future treatment of them by the German Nazis.

The *Anchluss* produced a short-lived honeymoon in Austria. Five years of constant tension, civil war, incessant propaganda, and acts of terrorism were at last over. The response resembled that following the outbreak of the First World War: general relief that the dreaded day had come and gone. And Austria was once again a part of a great power.

For Germany, the *Anschluss* meant the addition of over 6.5 million people, or eight *Wehrmacht* divisions. Austria's industry and financial investments in southeastern Europe now belonged to Germany. The Reich's trading position with the Successor States, already powerful, became absolutely dominant. Strategically, the *Anschluss* left the Historic Provinces of Czechoslovakia virtually surrounded by German territory; Czech access to its Little Entente ally, Yugoslovia, could be cut off at a moment's notice. Germany gained common borders with Hungary, Yugoslavia, and Italy, all of which now moved closer to the German orbit.

Western acquiescence in the *Anschluss* intensified the growing impression throughout Europe that Germany had been given a free hand in the Danube. Nazi parties among German minorities in East Central Europe grew in size and self-confidence. Britain and France responded by accelerating their rearmament programs, but only time would tell whether the effort was soon enough or massive enough.

Henlein, Hitler, and the Czechoslovak "Aircraft Carrier"

Nowhere were the consequences of the *Anschluss* more profound than in Czechoslovakia. The Sudeten Germans, their luxury industries devastated by the Great Depression and the decline in international trade, were suffering from an unemployment rate far higher than that found in Czech districts. But the Czechs, including the government in Prague, were as ignorant of Sudeten conditions as prewar Sudetens had been of the Czech sense of oppression. Prague was slow to respond to the emergency. The result was a growing Nazi movement in German areas which by 1935 had become a serious force in Czechoslovak politics; after the *Anschluss* it nearly annihilated the other Sudeten parties. Elections held in German-speaking regions in May and June 1938 gave the Nazi front "Sudeten German party" (SdP) 91 percent of the Sudeten vote; only the Social Democrats and Communists survived the landslide. The swing to the SdP resulted from the idealistic goal of eliminating all party differences and fear that "race traitors" would be severely punished once Hitler marched in.

Six weeks after the *Anchluss* the SdP, under the leadership of the young gymnastic instructor Konrad Henlein, announced eight demands at Karlsbad superficially intended to eliminate all Sudeten grievances accumulated since 1918. Sudeten Germans had to be granted equal status with the Czechs and autonomist rights resembling Hungary's after the *Ausgleich;* only economic and foreign affairs would remain under the jurisdiction of the central government, and in foreign affairs Czechoslovakia had to move into the German sphere of influence (just as before the war it had been the Czechs who had insisted that Austria-Hungary line up with the Triple Entente). In itself Henlein's program was no more extreme or unreasonable than prewar Czech ambitions. But unlike the Czechs of Imperial Austria the Sudetens no longer believed in the future existence of the state they lived in. Moreover, they were not bargaining in good faith. On March 28 Henlein had been personally ordered by Hitler to make demands higher than anything Prague could possibly concede.

Hitler, in fact, was using Henlein's party to destroy Czechoslovakia. By demanding first autonomy, then separation, while claiming to be "oppressed," the SdP would give the Führer a pretext for dismembering Czechoslovakia. This policy originated only in November 1937; until then Hitler would have been satisfied with *Gleichschaltung,* making Czechoslovakia a German satellite, the same status he envisaged for Poland, Hungary, Rumania, and Yugoslavia. But Beneš, while at first welcoming the secret offer of a nonaggression pact made by a German representative in the autumn of 1936, refused in 1937 to renounce his country's alliances with France and the Soviet Union.

Thereafter Hitler came to think of Czechoslovakia as an enemy "aircraft carrier." With thirty to forty well-trained and equipped divisions together with an air force two-thirds the size of the French, the Czechs threatened Germany's *drang nach Osten*. Czech air fields were within minutes of Munich, Nürnberg, Chemnitz, Leipzig, Dresden, and Breslau. But with Czechoslovakia in German hands, Nazi forces would nearly surround Hungary and Poland, would be poised on the border of Rumania, and would be within striking distance of the Soviet Union.

The strategic significance of Czechoslovakia was completely lost to most statesmen in the West, above all to those in Great Britain. Whereas before the war it had been their cardinal principle to prevent any one state from dominating the Continent, attention was now focused on redressing the "immoral" aspects of the peace treaties. British idealists had gone to war in 1914 to protect the rights of small nations; now they feared small states would drag them into an unwanted conflict. Doubts expressed by Lloyd George and others at the Peace Conference about the viability of new states all came rushing back in the middle thirties.

This lack of confidence in the Successor States encouraged a defensive mentality in the Western democracies. The outlook was manifested in the Locarno Pact, the building of the Maginot Line in northeastern France, and Anglo-French passivity toward Nazi treaty violations. France's offensive strategy took a beating in the international reaction against its occupation of Germany's industrial Ruhr district in 1923. Thereafter Paris counted on its eastern allies for aid in the event of a German attack, but never entertained the possibility of going to their assistance in case of a German thrust to the east. Germans had invaded France in 1792, 1814, 1870, and 1914; it was inconceivable they would not do so again. Britain would support France if such an invasion occurred. But what would the British do if there was no attack

in the West? Hitler had given his answer in 1924 in *Mein Kampf:*
The Kaiser's blunder, the Nazi leader maintained, was building
the German navy and invading Belgium and France; British
friendship could be won and France isolated if Germany's territorial ambitions were limited to the East.

The military strategy of Germany, France, and Britain
thus emasculated Czechoslovakia's alliances, on paper the
strongest in Central Europe. In 1935 the Czechs had signed a
defensive alliance with France and Russia. France would aid
Czechoslovakia in case of a German attack, after which the
Soviet Union would also intervene. But no provisions were made
for military consultations; hence there were no concrete dis-
cussions on how France and Russia would actually aid the
Czechoslovaks. When in May 1938 Beneš instructed his chief of
staff to consult the French about coordinating mobilization
plans, the French declined. Almost simultaneously the French
press denounced the possibility of French soldiers being used
as "cannon fodder" to defend Czechoslovakia.

Conversations between Chamberlain and the French premier, Edouard Daladier, held at the end of April 1938, revealed
Chamberlain to be equally reluctant to commit British troops
to foreign adventures. He, unlike Daladier, was sure Henlein
had no intention of destroying Czechoslovakia. In any event
he stressed that British military unpreparedness made assistance to Czechoslovakia impossible. Daladier refused to admit
that the situation was hopeless, but he was too weakwilled to
stand by his Czech ally.

The state of British armaments was only one of the considerations influencing Chamberlain's policy, and probably not
the most important. He knew that most Sudeten Germans favored joining the Reich. Should Great Britain now go to war
in order to frustrate the very principle of self-determination
for which the British had fought in World War I? He rightly
believed that the British would not gladly support such a struggle. Like Wilson and Mazzini before him, he was convinced that
realization of the nationality principle would further peace and
stability, not war. The cession of the Sudetenland to Germany,
upon which Chamberlain decided as early as May 1938, was

therefore not a tragic necessity, but a positive good. Exactly the same reasoning had influenced the Allied decision to dismember Austria-Hungary in 1918.

In a meeting with Hitler in Berchtesgaden (September 15) Chamberlain agreed to the direct transfer of Sudeten territory to the Reich. Czechoslovakia would also give up its military alliances in exchange for a general guarantee of the rest of the country against unprovoked aggression. This was the essence of an Anglo-French ultimatum delivered to the Czech government on the 21st. The Czechs knew that if they rejected the ultimatum they would face the Germans alone. Beneš's agonized consent turned Czech foreign policy over to the British and French, thereby sealing his country's fate. Austria was a horrible example of what happened to a small state lacking Western support. The vital importance of Czechoslovakia to the West had been a dogma for so long both in Prague and Paris that the Czech President could not imagine the West would ignore its own interests.

Beneš had one alternative: the acceptance of Soviet aid. The Russian ambassador in Prague assured him that even if France did not honor its alliance Russia would immediately respond to a Czech appeal to the League. Beneš was grateful for this offer, which went beyond Soviet obligations in the alliance of 1935. But after some hesitation he politely turned it down. Was he foolish? Probably not. Beneš could hardly ignore the recent fate of Spain, where Russian assistance in the civil war had alienated the West. Moreover, there had been no joint military planning with the Soviets, and the Czech General Staff, like Chamberlain, had no confidence in the ability of the Red Army after the purge of senior officers in 1937. Moreover, throughout the Sudeten crisis no military preparations took place in the Soviet Union; Stalin had no intention of aiding the Czechs and could not have done so even had he wanted to without Polish or Rumanian consent, neither of which was likely to be given.

Hitler was not satisfied with the mere transfer of the Sudetenland; only the complete disintegration of Czechoslovakia through the fulfillment of long-standing Hungarian and Polish claims would do. These were the new demands the Führer put to the British Prime Minister at their second meeting in Bad Godesberg. Chamberlain, as well as British and French public opinion, finally balked. War seemed inevitable. Czechoslovakia obstinately refused to collapse; the Slovaks did not attempt to secede and the Hungarians, instead of seizing the whole of Slovakia, issued only a mildly worded demand for Magyar districts, declining to threaten Prague with war. The navy-oriented and pro-British Horthy was careful to do nothing that might bring Hungary into conflict with Britain. Only Poland obliged Hitler with a belligerent posture; the Polish minority was instructed by Warsaw to follow Henlein's lead. Czechoslovakia's Little Entente ally Rumania adopted a "correct" attitude during the crisis, while Yugoslavia was sympathetic; but the two countries were willing to aid the Czechs only if the West did so as well. The Little Entente was acting like anything but a great power.

From Munich to Prague: The Liquidation of Czechoslovakia

Just when it appeared that a European war was unavoidable, Mussolini proposed a four-power conference. Everyone jumped at this opportunity to save face: Hitler could back away from a war which he realized would not be popular in Germany; Britain and France could appear to make concessions only after negotiations, not at the threat of force; Mussolini could avoid a war for which Italy was totally unprepared.

On September 29 Hitler, Chamberlain, Mussolini, and Daladier met in Munich to carve up Czechoslovakia "peacefully." The Czechs themselves were not represented and unlike the Austrians at St. Germain were not even allowed to make written protests. Significantly, the Poles and the Russians were also excluded. Incensed by this slight, Warsaw delivered an ultimatum to Prague on the 30th demanding (and getting) the return of Teschen. The Soviets, on the other hand, must have been delighted to escape responsibility for the partition and

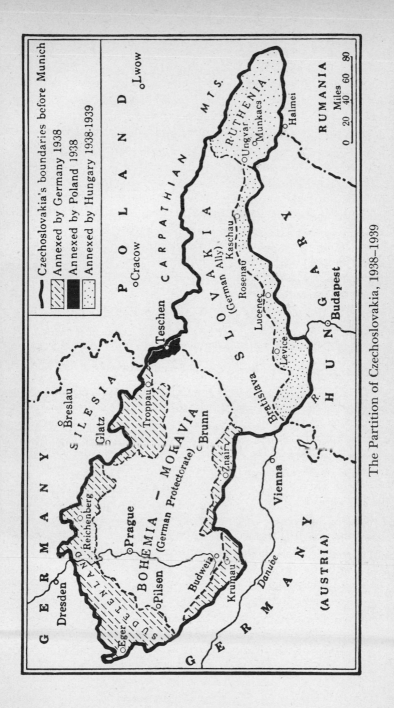

The Partition of Czechoslovakia, 1938–1939

rightly expected their noninvolvement to enhance their prestige in East Central Europe.

Hitler was given everything the British and French had been momentarily ready to fight for the day before. The only compromise—if it can be called that—was the German occupation of the Sudetenland in stages over a ten-day period instead of all at once as Hitler had earlier demanded. But the occupation was to take place before the new frontiers were delimited by an international commission. In practice the West was granting Germany the right to carry out *faits accomplis,* just as France had sanctioned Czech moves in 1918. The promised guarantee of a rump Czechoslovakia was not contained in the Munich Agreement, only a statement of intentions. Nor did the West seriously consider how the truncated Czech state could survive.

Hitler's only disappointment was not getting his war with Czechoslovakia. Critics who have maintained that a general war with Nazi Germany would have been preferable in 1938 rather than 1939 are both right and wrong. Right, because Germany was vulnerable to an attack from the West. Wrong, because the West never would have attacked Germany, and Czechoslovakia would have been left to perish like Poland less than a year later. Hitler could have been stopped in 1938, but not without a major war involving offensives by France, Britain, Poland, and Czechoslovakia. But the very thought of war was terrifying to Western statesmen.

The Munich Agreement was probably less important than the *Anschluss* in shifting the balance of power in East Central Europe in Hitler's favor. The 3.5 million people ceded to Germany were only half as numerous as the Austrians and lived in territories farther removed from the Danube. The swing to the Right in both domestic and foreign policies as well as German economic penetration of southeastern Europe were intensified but not initiated by Munich. Only in Rumania did the Agreement produce a decisive shift in policies. The West lost still more influence in East Central Europe, but little had been left to lose after the *Anschluss.*

For the West itself, however, Munich was far more serious

than the *Anschluss.* There had been no formal alliances with Austria or even guarantees of its integrity—only diplomatic statements of sympathy. Versailles and St. Germain were violated by the annexation, but they had been violated before. The disappearance of democracy, the violent suppression of the Socialist party, and the German culture of the people had made it psychologically and morally easier for the West to write off the Austrians. No such pretext existed for Czechoslovakia. After sighs of relief at the avoidance of war, many in the West began to realize that a strong, democratic, and loyal ally had been left in the lurch. Consciences began hurting.

As for Czechoslovakia, Munich was an unmitigated catastrophe, albeit not necessarily for the reasons commonly supposed. Even with the loss of 200,000 people to Poland and upward of another million to Hungary in the "First Vienna Award" in November, Czechoslovakia still had nearly 10 million souls in two-thirds of its former territory. Adequate industry and natural resources were left to the Republic, and in agriculture it was now self-sufficient. A modest economic consolidation even took place in the first months after Munich. Compared to the boundaries left to Austria and Hungary at Paris the Czechoslovaks were economically fortunate indeed. American newspapers editorialized optimistically that Czechoslovakia was better off without its Sudeten population.

A more satisfactory relationship was worked out between majority nationalities when Slovaks and Ruthenes were given their long-denied local autonomy. Czechoslovakia became "Czecho-Slovakia" just as the Habsburg Monarchy became hyphenated in the Austro-Hungarian Compromise of 1867. The compromise of 1938 resembled the old *Ausgleich* in leaving only foreign affairs, national defense, and national finance in the hands of the central government. Twenty years after the fall of Austria-Hungary, Czechoslovakia together with Yugoslavia thus ironically returned to the structure of the Dual Monarchy.

But these developments only masked the true nature of the Czechoslovak calamity. After the German occupation of the Sudetenland, 738,500 Czechs were transferred to Germany, while only 234,000 Germans were left in the Historic Provinces.

The boundaries were drawn in such a way that nearly 300,000 Czechs were needlessly annexed, and the remainder of the country was left defenseless. Czechs now faced not a *gemütlich,* middle-sized south German state, as could have been the case after 1919, but a Nazi powerhouse with some 75 million people. The Czechs had no choice but to reorientate their domestic and internal policies to the Right, as most other Successor States had done after the *Anschluss.* Parties of the Left were dissolved and convinced democrats resigned their offices, including President Beneš. Mildly anti-Semitic laws were enacted to appease the Nazis still further. The alliance with Russia was formally renounced, and the French military mission in Prague quietly packed up and went home. The promised international guarantees were never formally concluded. Czecho-Slovakia was a German satellite.

Five months after Munich a constitutional crisis arose in Czecho-Slovakia. Slovak and Ruthenian fascists insisted on complete independence, just as had Magyar extremists after 1867 and Croatian hotbloods in 1939. The Slovakian movement was home grown, but Hitler was more than willing to take advantage of it. On March 9, 1939, Prague, erroneously believing the autonomous government in Bratislava was about to declare independence, dismissed the Slovak prime minister, Josef Tiso, along with most of his cabinet. Tiso was summoned to Berlin where the Führer gave him the choice between independence and annexation by Hungary. On March 14 the Slovak Diet dutifully, if unenthusiastically, voted for independence. Ruthenia (now called the "Sub-Carpatho-Ukraine") followed suit, but was occupied within twenty-four hours by Hungary. Using nonexistent Czech atrocities against the tiny German minority as a pretext, German troops occupied Bohemia and Moravia on the 15th. What remained of Czech independence was dead.

Both the Czechs and Slovaks were brought under the "protection" of Nazi Germany and allowed to retain some autonomy. Slovakia was nominally independent, but with a foreign policy coordinated to Germany's. It had to allow German troops on its soil and even to permit German exploitation of its natural resources. Hitler gained Czech army stocks, Europe's second largest armaments factory (the famous Skoda munition works in Pilsen), and the elimination of the Czech army. And now Poland and Hungary were strategically at his mercy.

Hungarian Revisionism

Meanwhile, Hungary was desperately trying to profit from Nazi Germany's drive to rearrange the map of Europe while at the same time avoiding the fate of Austria and Czechoslovakia. It was to be a losing battle.

The right-wing prime minister, General Gyula Gömbös (1932–1935), although Hitler's admirer in many respects, tried to keep Hungary out of the Führer's clutches by attaching his country to Italy and Austria in the Rome Protocols of March 1934. Other premiers sought a rapprochement with the Little Entente in exchange for territorial concessions or closer relations with the West. But by 1939 Austria had disappeared, the Little Entente was dead, and the West had no interest in Hungary. Prime Minister Paul Teleki tried to revive the Italian tie in 1939, but by this late date Mussolini had conceded the Danube basin to Hitler.

Hungary's only other hope of staying out of the German orbit lay in joining an East European power bloc stretching from the Baltic to the Black Sea. But the possibility for such an alliance was ruined by the First Vienna Award of November 2, 1938, in which Hitler blocked the establishment of a common Polish-Hungarian border in Ruthenia by limiting Hungarian territorial gains in the disputed border with Slovakia to the southern Magyar fringe. The long-coveted access to Poland was finally achieved with the total disintegration of Czechoslovakia in March 1939, when Hungary annexed the Ruthenes of the Sub-Carpatho-Ukraine. But the Hungarian move was accompanied by the German military occupation of Slovakia. Germany was now too powerful to be resisted by any East European combination.

Hungary later managed to regain further pieces of the prewar kingdom in the Second Vienna Award of August 1940, when Germany and Italy granted it the northern two-fifths of

Transylvania; in 1941 it reannexed part of northern Yugoslavia after that country had been routed by a German *Blitzkrieg*. Hungary's power position vis-à-vis Germany, however, far from improving, actually deteriorated. And Germany's aid in regaining the lost territories only reinforced the impression, widespread in the West, that Hungary was a willing German satellite. A satellite Hungary undoubtedly was, but certainly not a willing one. If Budapest had stood up to the Nazis after 1938, it would have met the fate in store for Warsaw in the fall of 1939. As it was, Hungary managed to stay out of the Second World War for a time, but only until the German attack on Russia. In the end it was conquered by the Soviets and stripped of its recent gains.

Poland and the Outbreak of World War II

Hungary was always something of a bad boy in Western eyes for not complacently accepting Trianon. But Poland, for many years, was in high favor west of the Rhine, an attitude not always reciprocated by the proud Poles.

Poland had been alienated from the West as early as 1925 when it was virtually excluded from the Locarno Conference; French willingness in 1933 to forego Polish participation in a European directorate known as the Four-Power Pact cooled Polish opinion of Paris almost to the freezing point. France's rejection of Pilsudski's offer to join France in a preventative war against Nazi Germany shortly after Hitler came to power did little to improve relations between the two countries.

Partly as an act of defiance and self-assertion, but partly because of the feeble French policy toward Germany, the Polish dictator signed a nonaggression pact with Germany in 1934. On the surface Poland profited handsomely. Germany terminated its campaign for revision in the Corridor, put a stop to a tariff war with Poland, and moderated its support for the German minority. If nothing else, Poland had presumably gained ten years to put its house in order and had demonstrated its ability to pursue an independent foreign policy. Less obvious, however, was the weakening of its already decrepit ties with the

West. The almost simultaneous denunciation of Poland's minority treaty contributed still further to the decline of the country's international standing.

An opportunity for better relations with the West appeared in March 1936 with Germany's illegal remilitarization of the Rhineland. Foreign Minister Józef Beck offered to cooperate with France in forcefully resisting the German move; but again the answer from Paris was in the negative. Thereafter Poland tended to drift toward the revisionist powers, Italy and Hungary, while staying on friendly terms with Nazi Germany. Beck was unconcerned by the *Anschluss,* assuming it only proved Hitler's interest in southeastern Europe. The same thought prevailed during the Munich crisis. Poland's anxiety to seize Teschen, if necessary by force, helped to discourage France from taking military action.

Colonel Beck was hardly a farsighted statesman in the Munich crisis or on many other occasions. But neither was he exactly the vulture depicted in the West. He had offered Beneš an alliance in 1933 but was turned down. Polish support for a united front against Germany could still have been gained in 1938 by a timely Western guarantee of Czechoslovak independence or an early Czech territorial concession to Poland. When neither was forthcoming and it became clear that the West would not fight for Czechoslovakia, Beck scurried to save something from the debacle by occupying Teschen.

Beck's foreign policy was built on two premises, both of them false: (1) Germany had no political ambitions in Poland, and (2) even if it did, Poland would be strong enough to defend itself. The first clue to Germany's true intentions came on October 24, 1938, less than four weeks after Munich. The Nazi foreign minister, Joachim von Ribbentrop, proposed to the Polish ambassador that Danzig revert to the Reich, Germany be given extraterritorial connections across the Corridor to East Prussia, the nonaggression pact be extended, and Poland adhere to the anti-Comintern Pact against Russia. Essentially, Ribbentrop was proposing that Poland become a German dependency. Poland's helpful policy during the Munich crisis gave the Nazis reason to suppose it would welcome such a status. The Poles

politely declined Ribbentrop's offer and German-Polish relations remained unaltered—for the time being. Then, after the
Nazi occupation of Bohemia and Moravia, Ribbentrop renewed
his offer (March 21, 1939), this time using a menacing tone, but
hinting that Polish compliance might be rewarded in Slovakia.
When Beck again refused, the German foreign minister adopted
a still more threatening attitude. Two days after this interview
Germany occupied the partly German-speaking district of Lith-
uania known as Memelland. The Polish government now feared
that Danzig would be next.

Meanwhile, British foreign policy was undergoing a revolution. Hitler's occupation of Prague in mid-March had left
Chamberlain feeling betrayed. He had convinced himself that
Hitler was an honest, if rather crude, man who wanted nothing
more than to right the wrongs of Versailles and incorporate
fellow Germans into the Reich. The occupation of almost purely
Czech territories demolished this illusion. Hitler's word, it was
clear, could no longer be trusted. The English leader now rushed
to promise Poland, with its long, exposed German frontier,
everything he had denied the Czechoslovak fortress. Hitler's
demands on Poland were modest compared to those he made
in the case of the Sudetenland. But it was with dictatorial Poland, not democratic Czechoslovakia, that the Prime Minister
chose to make his stand. On March 31, 1939, he announced to the
House of Commons a guarantee of Poland's independence.

Chamberlain's change of heart came too late. Nazi Germany already controlled Central and East Central Europe,
either directly or indirectly. While the British had been concerned with morality, Hitler had been concerned with conquest
and power. When the British finally realized that morality was
no longer the real issue, it was too late to shift the balance back
in their favor without a major war. Appeasement had to be tested
to be proved right or wrong. But once proved wrong there was
no alternative to war.

The British had no way of defending Poland and did not
even plan to. The guarantee was merely a diplomatic deterrent.
Hitler refused to take it seriously. Why would the British defend Poland when they had abandoned Czechoslovakia? The

Reich Chancellor had no desire for war with the West but was prepared to accept one if Britain and France insisted. So British threats in the spring and summer of 1939 were useless.

When the Poles continued to turn down a satellite status, Germany declared war on September 1. Chamberlain dared not back down on his pledge lest his government lose what little remained of its credibility. For the same reason Russia had been unable to relinquish its protection of Serbia in 1914. The last of the "insurmountable barriers" was about to fall, and for the second time in twenty-five years East Central Europe provided the explosives which the great powers used to set off a world war.

CHAPTER SIX

Looking Back

The collapse of the Paris Settlement after only twenty years has caused historians to re-evaluate the character of the Habsburg Monarchy and the concept of national self-determination. What to some observers before 1914 looked like an oppressive, corrupt, and reactionary regime, now looks tolerant, honest, enlightened, and even progressive in comparison to what followed. No one but a confirmed romantic would contend that the Monarchy was without serious problems and faults, but even the harsh critic A. J. P. Taylor has admitted that

> There was equality before the law, civil marriage, freedom of expression, freedom of movement. . . . There were balanced budgets and stable currency for more than thirty years. . . . The police state of Metternich still existed, but . . . it was a police

state exposed to public criticism and confined to civilized be-
havior. The Austrian citizen after 1867 had more civic security
than the German and was in the hands of more honest and capable officials than in France or Italy. . . .[1]

Although it is clear that numerous disgruntled national
and social elements existed within the Monarchy, it no longer
seems so obvious just what the Habsburgs could have done without worsening the situation. It is more than doubtful whether
this or that alteration of provincial boundaries, this or that
constitutional change, or this or that cession of irredentist territory to a neighboring nation-state could have "saved" the Empire and ended internal strife. As the First World War and Peace
Conference showed, the ambitions of the Austro-Hungarian
nationalities and the bordering states were not confined to ethnic
justice, but were imperialistic—aiming at domination of neighboring nationalities. The Magyars were granted more than
equality in 1867, yet remained unpacified. The Czechs were
offered equality in 1890, but rejected it in favor of the lopsided
gains of 1918–1919. The Italian Kingdom rejected Austria's
1915 offer of ethnic equality in the Trentino in favor of the
Treaty of London.

Complete ethnic justice in the Habsburg Monarchy was
impeded by a delicate internal balance of power. Hungary could
checkmate Austria; the Emperor could checkmate the Magyars.
The German Bohemians were strong enough to block the Bohemian Czechs' *Staatsrecht* program, while the Czechs were in
a position to prevent the partition of Bohemia along ethnic
lines. The domestic power balance prevented reform, but it also
stood in the way of oppression. Where the balance did not exist,
as within Hungary, or to a lesser extent Galicia, real discrimination against minorities did exist. What the war and Peace Conference did was to destroy the balance and to leave one nationality in each new state in a position to lord it over new national
minorities.

How long the internal balance and the existence of the

---

[1] *The Habsburg Monarchy, 1809–1918: A History of the Austrian Empire and
Austria-Hungary* (New York: Harper & Row, 1965), pp. 138–139.

Monarchy itself could have lasted is an unanswerable question. It is hard to imagine, however, that either could have been disrupted without a major crisis like a war or possibly drastic, overhasty reforms. States in being do not suddenly collapse of their own weight. The First World War upset the balance of power both within the Monarchy and within Europe as a whole. All those nineteenth-century movements incompatible with the existence of the Habsburg state were intensified by the war. Nationalism, republicanism, and democracy were victorious; any one of them was capable of destroying the dual state.

In the early years of the war the Western democracies could not readily exploit the ideologies they represented, because of their alliance with Tsarist Russia. But once the Tsar was overthrown, and once it became increasingly apparent that Austria-Hungary could neither be defeated by orthodox military measures nor separated from its German ally by diplomacy, the only remaining way to eliminate it from the Central Alliance was by encouraging independence movements among the smaller nationalities.

It would be entirely misleading, of course, to suggest that Allied psychological warfare and diplomacy were solely responsible for the demise of the Monarchy; they were simply the final catalysts. To a large extent the collapse came because Austro-Hungarian and German arms succeeded too well. Since its emergence as a great power in 1526, the Habsburg Monarchy had been essentially a defensive federation of nationalities. Until the eighteenth century the Ottoman Empire had been the hereditary foe; thereafter it was the Russians. During the first half of the Great War Austria-Hungary was a besieged fortress surrounded on nearly every side by greedy enemies: Russia, Serbia, Italy, and finally Rumania. Yet by 1917 these states were either defeated or on the defensive. A year later, Germany, the bugaboo of the Austro-Slavic nationalities, was also nearing the end of its military strength. The *raison d'être* of the Monarchy seemed to have disappeared.

Equally fatal to the Monarchy was modernization. Nationalism is usually cited as the overriding centrifugal force in Austria-Hungary. In fact, nationalism was but one aspect of modernization. Modern secularism undermined the position of the Roman Catholic Church, one of the Monarchy's great pillars. Industrialization and urbanization aggravated relations between social classes and nationalities. Modern rationalism made the legitimist, divine right theory of monarchy look ridiculously anachronistic. Modern parliamentarianism and advanced methods of communications only increased contact and therewith friction between Habsburg nationalities.

The First World War came at the worst possible stage of the modernization process for the Habsburg Monarchy. Industry and democracy had developed far enough to disrupt the traditional peasant-monarchical structure of the state, but had not matured enough to establish stable new traditions. Given another generation or two of peace and economic progress, the Monarchy's nationalities might have reached near economic, social, and political equality, thus conceivably diminishing national hostility.

To the Allies, the breakup of the multinational empire and self-determination for its ethnic groups were the very essence of modernity. And yet they forgot that while the creation of nation-states had been one dominant theme in the nineteenth century, another had been the establishment of larger and economically more efficient states. The outcome of the war and the Paris Settlement reversed the latter trend by creating small, often economically backward, and militarily weak states.

Except for a few hard-core monarchists—German-Austrian aristocrats, politically conservative Catholics, and members of the former Austro-Hungarian military elite—the passing of the Habsburg Monarchy was little mourned. Anyone with the slightest claim to being liberal, democratic, nationalistic, or progressive greeted its downfall as the start of a new age of freedom and enlightenment.

But the West had cause to regret the Monarchy's disappearance already at the Paris Peace Conference. Instead of treating with just one foreign office, the Allies now had to deal with separate governments in Austria, Hungary, and Czechoslovakia, not to mention Poland and the enlarged Balkan states.

The fate of the German Austrians, virtually forgotten in

wartime diplomacy, loomed as one of the Big Four's major headaches. Having proclaimed self-determination as an inalienable right, the Western Powers nevertheless were forced into the morally indefensible position of compelling 10 million Habsburg Germans in Czechoslovakia and Austria to live in states which most of them repudiated. It is hardly a wonder that they became frustrated and embittered.

The West was later to learn that self-determination, like the related principle of popular sovereignty, could not be easily limited or qualified. If it was really a universal and inalienable right, then it had to be extended to all who demanded it. Self-determination was a useful tool in breaking up the Habsburg Monarchy and defeating the Central Powers; as a state-building device it was far less practical, at least in East Central Europe. Moreover, it could not be monopolized by the West. Hitler seized it to undermine Western interest in Austrian independence and to strip Czechoslovakia of its natural defenses. Britain was trapped into submitting in part by its own idealism.

Even before the Nazi occupation of Austria and Czechoslovakia the denial of self-determination to new postwar minorities was undermining the stability and democratic institutions of the Secessionist States. Stuffed with huge, resentful minorities these states responded with repressive measures that only poisoned domestic politics. A vicious circle ensued with democracy the chief loser.

In none of the Successor States, except Czechoslovakia—and scarcely even there—did a broad popular consensus exist in favor of the state, its constitution, or its government. In Yugoslavia the three dominant nationalities could reach no agreement on these fundamental issues. Poland and Rumania had large, dissatisfied minorities, and even the majority nationalities were divided politically. Austria was split socially and politically. Only Hungary was reasonably homogeneous nationally and politically, but there the social question and the absence of democratic traditions prevented the development of genuinely representative institutions.

Special problems created by the legacy of the war, the Peace Conference, or national development, existed in all the

Successor States. In both Hungary and Austria the overthrow of the old autocratic regimes, accompanied as it was by military defeat, national humiliation in the peace treaties, and the rise of militant Socialism and Communism, prejudiced the new democratic order in the eyes of conservatives and many moderates. The Secessionist States were handicapped by untrained and corrupt bureaucracies, selfish and irresponsible ruling classes, unbalanced economies, a superabundance of quarreling political parties, and overly ambitious foreign policies. Only Czechoslovakia stood out as a partial exception.

Democracy can function smoothly only where there is agreement on fundamentals, where at least a substantial majority is willing to abide by the rules of the political game. Differences between political factions arise over tactics and the details of practical programs, but these differences are regarded as less important than the common good. Those in power must rule for the benefit of all, not merely their own constituency, and the opposition must be willing to wait its turn to come to power by legal, peaceful means. These conditions simply did not exist in the Successor States, or to a sufficient degree in the last years of prewar Austria. Every party and ethnic group was loyal only to itself and in the Successor States regarded rivals as mortal enemies who had to be denied access to power. No substitute was found for the Habsburgs as the supreme object of political loyalty.

Divided within, nationally, socially, and politically, and internationally by innumerable boundary disputes, the Successor States were unable to play the role expected of them by the West in 1918–1919, that of a barrier to great power imperialism. Austria, the most artificial of the states of East Central Europe, was the first to disappear. The role of the West in this event was curious, to say the least. In 1919, when the Austrian people almost universally desired a union with Germany, a union that might have influenced German politics in a way favorable to democracy, the West balked. Again in 1931, when the faltering democratic governments of Germany and Austria might have benefited from a customs union, the French resolutely vetoed even that. In 1938, however, when most Austrians no longer favored an *Anschluss* that would enormously strengthen the military-strategic position of an aggressive and unpredictable Nazi Germany, the West raised only the feeblest paper protest. The rationalization often cited for this passivity was Austria's post-1933 authoritarian regime. Yet by the autumn of 1938 the West also left democratic Czechoslovakia in the lurch. A new excuse was found in the case of the Czech state, namely the country's heterogeneous ethnic composition. Hitler exploited this issue to partition Czechoslovakia, just as the Allies had done in encouraging the disintegration of Austria-Hungary.

The Habsburg Monarchy lasted 400 years as a multinational state. Czechoslovakia and Yugoslavia, the two states most resembling the Monarchy, survived scarcely two decades. It required four years of grueling warfare to break up Austria-Hungary; only a conference and the threat of war were needed to partition the Czechoslovak Republic. A few weeks of war sufficed to dissolve the Yugoslav Kingdom.

Shortly after the end of the Second World War, Winston Churchill, himself an early proponent of Austria-Hungary's dismemberment, wrote: "There is not one of the peoples or provinces of the Empire of the Hapsburgs to whom gaining their independence has not brought the tortures which ancient poets and theologians had reserved for the damned."[2] Since 1914 East Central Europe has been the plaything of the great powers. First Imperial Germany dominated Austria-Hungary and the Balkans during the First World War. Then France and Italy competed for control of the Successor States, with France securing the support of the "victors" and Italy turning the vanquished into satellites. After 1936 all the states of East Central Europe gravitated into the orbit of Nazi Germany. Following World War II it was Soviet Russia's turn to control most of the area.

With foreign domination has come a succession of doctrinaire theories. At the end of the First World War the theory of national self-determination was employed in the partition of

---

[2] *The Second World War*, Vol. I, *The Gathering Storm* (Boston: Houghton Mifflin, 1948), p. 9.

the area into what became feuding states. In the late thirties the Nazi theory of *Lebensraum* (living space) was used to justify Hitler's conquests. During the Second World War Nazi racial theories led to the extermination of the most culturally creative of the Danube nationalities, the Jews. Shortly after the war racial and national theories were again utilized in the expulsion of the region's economically most productive nationality, the ethnic Germans. Marxist dogmas were imposed on the survivors of earlier disasters—and from this most recent blight the area has yet to recover. Each theory was utopian in its own way, and each brought fresh calamities. Each new regime fanatically strove to eliminate all traces of its predecessor's ideology. National self-determination was no doubt the mildest of these theories, yet it opened the way for the later, more vicious ones by destroying the Habsburg Monarchy and its tolerant, humane traditions.

Of the Habsburg nationalities only the German Austrians have today recovered the freedom which others lost just before or during the Second World War. Those nationalities "liberated from the yoke of Habsburg oppression" now suffer from a denial of personal liberty unimaginable in the old Monarchy.

Bibliographical Note

There is no book, aside from the present one, which compares the fate of East Central Europe immediately before and after the First World War. Broader in geographical scope and chronology is Alan Palmer's factual textbook, *The Lands Between, A History of East-Central Europe since the Congress of Vienna* (New York: The Macmillan Company, 1970). Students of the subject are fortunate in having at their disposal the *Austrian History Yearbook,* which since 1965 has published excellent articles on the Habsburg Monarchy, the Republic of Austria, and Trianon Hungary by scholars in both the United States and Europe. Volume III for 1967, in three parts, is invaluable for its discussion of the causes of the Dual Monarchy's downfall. An earlier periodical dealing in part with East Central Europe is the *Journal of Central European Affairs* (1941–1964). Useful articles can also be found in the semipopular Austrian journal, *Österreich in Geschichte und Literatur.*

Of the more general works on East Central Europe, a thoughtful and warmly pro-Austrian history of the Habsburg Monarchy and the two Austrian republics is Gordon Brook-Shepherd, *The Austrian Odyssey* (London: Macmillan & Co., Ltd., 1957). Published too late for use in this study is William M. Johnston's pioneering work, *The Austrian Mind, An Intellectual and Social History, 1848–1938* (Berkeley and Los Angeles: University of California Press, 1971). The Hungarian-American historian, Stephen Borsody, has made an eloquent plea for federalism in the Danube basin in *The Tragedy of Central Europe

*Asterisks denote books in paperback editions.

(New York: Crowell-Collier and Macmillan, Inc., 1960) which concentrates on Hungary and Czechoslovakia since 1918. Passionately pro-Czech and anti-Habsburg is S. Harrison Thomson's *Czechoslovakia in European History* (Hamden, Conn.: Archon Books, 1965; first published in 1943), which is admirably comprehensive, but somewhat dated. Far more objective, but much narrower in breadth is Elizabeth Wiskemann, *Czechs and Germans,* 2d ed. (New York: St. Martin's Press, Inc., 1967; first published in 1938).

On the Austrian Empire the latest and most detailed account is Carlile A. Macartney, *The Habsburg Monarchy, 1790–1918* (New York: The Macmillan Company, 1969). Like most general studies of the Monarchy it tends to concentrate on politics to the detriment of cultural and intellectual developments. It is enlightening on economic changes, however, and contains an excellent annotated bibliography. The dualistic period is covered best by Arthur J. May's prize-winning book, *The Habsburg Monarchy, 1867–1914* (New York: W. W. Norton & Company, Inc., 1968; first published in 1951). Descriptive and factual rather than analytical, it is particularly useful on foreign policy where it proves that the Ballhausplatz was much less subservient to Berlin than was once commonly supposed. A colorful, but not always reliable history of the Monarchy is provided by the English journalist Edward Crankshaw in *The Fall of the House of Habsburg* (New York: The Viking Press, Inc., 1963). Despite its title, the book covers the period between 1848 and 1918, focusing on the life of Franz Joseph. A highly critical and opinionated study is Alan J. P. Taylor, *The Habsburg Monarchy, 1809–1918: A History of the Austrian Empire and Austria-Hungary* (New York: Harper & Row, Publishers, Inc., Harper Torchbook, 1965; first published in 1948). Perhaps the best descriptive work on the Monarchy by an eyewitness is Henry Wickham Steed, *The Habsburg Monarchy* (New York: Charles Scribner's Sons, 1913), which is critical, but not hostile. The best general study of the Monarchy by an Austrian scholar is Hugo Hantsch, *Die Geschichte Österreichs,* vol. II, *1648–1918* (Graz: Verlag Styria, 1953), which is markedly pro-Habsburg.

On more specialized topics an excellent analysis of the nationality problem is presented by Hantsch in *Die Nationalitätenfrage im Alten Österreich* (Vienna: Herold, 1953). A classic study of the centripetal and centrifugal forces at work in the Dual Monarchy is Oscar Jaszi, *The Dissolution of the Habsburg Monarchy* (Chicago: University of Chicago Press, Phoenix Books, 1961; first published in 1929). The Austro-American historian Robert A. Kann has given us two first-rate analytical studies of nationalism in *The Habsburg Empire, A Study in*

Integration and Disintegration (New York: Frederick A. Praeger, Inc., 1957) and *The Multinational Empire, Nationalism and National Reform in the Habsburg Monarchy, 1848–1918,* 2 vols. (New York: Columbia University Press, 1950). Kann believes that the Kremsier constitution of 1848 provided the best opportunity for successful reform but maintains that the collapse of the Monarchy without war was no certainty. The best biography of Franz Joseph is still Joseph Redlich, *Emperor Francis Joseph of Austria, A Biography* (Hamden, Conn.: Archon Books, 1965; first published in 1929), which is sympathetic but not uncritical. Very hostile, but not without insight, is Anatol Murad, *Franz Joseph I of Austria and His Empire* (New York: Twayne Publishers, Inc., 1968).

The standard works on the origins of the First World War are Luigi Albertini, *The Origins of the War of 1914,* 3 vols. (London: Oxford University Press, 1952–1957), which is exhaustive, but practically unreadable; Sidney B. Fay, **The Origins of the World War,* 2 vols. (New York: The Free Press, 1966; first published in 1928) excuses the Central Powers of sole responsibility for the war; Bernadotte E. Schmitt, *The Coming of the War, 1914* (New York: Howard Fertig, Inc., 1966; first published in 1930), pins most of the guilt on Germany; and Alan J. P. Taylor, *The Struggle for Mastery in Europe, 1848–1918* (Oxford: Clarendon Press, 1957). Two briefer and more recent works based on secondary sources are Laurence Lafore, **The Long Fuse, An Interpretation of the Origins of World War I* (Philadelphia: J. B. Lippincott Co., 1965), which focuses on the Balkan problem; and Joachim Remak, **The Origins of World War I* (New York: Holt, Rinehart and Winston, Inc., 1967), which stresses the vital importance of the Sarajevo assassination. For details of the assassination see Remak's *Sarajevo* (New York: Criterion Books, Inc., 1959) and Vladimir Dedijer, *The Road to Sarajevo* (New York: Simon and Schuster, Inc., 1966), which is exhaustive, but violently anti-Habsburg and Marxist. Most histories of the First World War concentrate on military events and by now are rather dated. For a recent interpretive study see A. J. P. Taylor's **A History of the First World War* (New York: Berkley Publishing Corporation, 1963).

Several meritorious works have been written on Austria-Hungary in the World War. The most recent and encyclopedic is Arthur J. May, *The Passing of the Hapsburg Monarchy, 1914–1918,* 2 vols. (Philadelphia: University of Pennsylvania Press, 1966). A sound work on the role of the Austro-Slavs in the Monarchy's disintegration is Z. A. B. Zeman, *The Break-up of the Habsburg Empire, A Study of National and Social Revolution* (London: Oxford University Press, 1961). A fascinating eyewitness description of the effects of the war on Austro-Hungarian society is found in Wolf von Schierbrand, *Austria-Hungary, The Polyglot Empire* (New York: Frederick A. Stokes, 1917). The impact of wartime economic exhaustion on the political structure of the Monarchy is described by David Mitrany in *The Effect of the War in Southeastern Europe* (New Haven, Conn.: Yale University Press, 1936).

Narrower studies on the wartime Monarchy include Joseph Redlich, *Austrian War Government* (New Haven, Conn.: Yale University Press, 1929), which is extremely critical of Austria's military dictatorship. Victor S. Mamatey, in *The United States and East-Central Europe, 1914-1918; A Study in Wilsonian Diplomacy and Propaganda* (Princeton, N.J.: Princeton University Press, 1957), explains Wilson's role in the breakup of the Monarchy and proves conclusively that the President began working for Austro-Hungary's dismemberment only in the late spring of 1918. The best account in English of the performance of the Imperial and Royal army is Edmund von Glaise-Horstenau, *The Collapse of the Austro-Hungarian Empire* (London: J. M. Dent & Sons, Ltd., 1930), which is sympathetic to the Central Powers, but not uncritical of German military policies. A good example of wartime propaganda carried out by the Austro-Hungarian exiles is Edouard Beneš, *Bohemia's Case for Independence* (London: George Allen & Unwin, Ltd., 1917), in which the future Czechoslovak President fails to mention the existence of the Sudeten Germans. The brief reign of the Emperor-King Karl is described by Reinhold Lorenz in *Kaiser Karl und der Untergang der Donaumonarchie* (Graz: Verlag Styria, 1959), which is detailed but based primarily on secondary sources. See also Gordon Brook-Shepherd, *The Last Habsburg* (New York: Weybright and Talley, Inc., 1968), a colorful, but uncritical account.

The Paris Peace Conference has produced an enormous literature, but mainly devoted to the Treaty of Versailles. The most complete, albeit rather dated work is still Harold V. W. Temperley (ed.), *A History of the Peace Conference of Paris*, 6 vols. (London: Oxford University Press, 1969; first published, 1920-1924). Volumes IV and V deal largely with East Central and Southeastern Europe. Karl R. Stadler, *The Birth of the Austrian Republic, 1918-1921* (Leyden: A. W. Sjthoff, 1966), gives a thorough treatment of the Treaty of St. Germain. A documentary collection of the same treaty can be found in Nina Almond and Ralph H. Lutz (eds.), *The Treaty of St. Germain: A Documentary History of the Territorial and Political Clauses with a Survey of the Documents of the Supreme Council of the Paris Peace Conference* (Stanford, Calif.: Stanford University Press, 1935).

On the Treaty of Trianon see Francis Deak, *Hungary at the Paris Peace Conference* (New York: Columbia University Press, 1942), which is marred by the author's failure to mention the Magyars' prewar policies toward their minorities. Ivo J. Lederer covers the Yusoslav role in his *Yugoslavia at the Paris Peace Conference: A Study in Frontiermaking* (New Haven, Conn.: Yale University Press, 1963), which is not entirely objective on the Austrian boundary. A little known but superb study of Czechoslovakia at the Peace Conference is Dagmar H. Perman, *The Shaping of the Czechoslovak State: Diplomatic History of the Boundaries of Czechoslovakia* (Leiden: E. J. Brill, 1962). Perman maintains that Britain and the United States lacked an overall plan for postwar East Central Europe thus enabling France to push through its program of building potential allies with supposedly strong, strategic frontiers. How Italy acquired the southwestern portions of the Habsburg Monarchy is explained in René Albrecht-Carrié, *Italy at the Peace Conference* (Hamden, Conn.: Archon Books, 1966; first published in 1938). Rumania's exploitation of the Red Scare of 1919 is revealed by Sherman D. Spector in *Rumania at the Paris Peace Conference: A Study of the Diplomacy of I. C. Bratianu* (New York: Twayne Publishers, Inc., 1962). A fuller study of Allied reaction to Bolshevism at this time is Arno J. Mayer, **Politics and Diplomacy of Peacemaking: Containment and Counterrevolution at Versailles, 1918–1919* (New York: Alfred A. Knopf, Inc., 1967). One of the British commissioners at the Conference, Harold Nicolson, has written a charming and revealing book about the hopes and prejudices of the treaty makers in **Peacemaking 1919* (New York: Grosset & Dunlap, Inc., 1965; first published in 1933).

The history of the Successor States in the interwar years is described in countless works, most of which are partisan, polemical, nationalistic, or panegyric. An exception is C. A. Macartney and A. W. Palmer, **Independent Eastern Europe, A History* (New York: St. Martin's Press, Inc., 1966; first published in 1962), which is also the only general historical survey of the area for these decades. Detailed and factual, it is weak on analysis, but contains an exhaustive bibliographical essay. A somewhat dated study which, however, is still useful on economic and social conditions is Hugh Seton-Watson, **Eastern Europe between the Wars, 1918–1941* (New York: Harper & Row, Publishers, Inc., Harper Torchbook, 3d rev. ed., 1967; first published in 1945). The disastrous economic impact of Austria-Hungary's disappearance is revealed in Frederick Hertz, *The Economic Problems of the Danubian States: A Study in Economic Nationalism* (London: V. Gollancz, 1947) and Leo Pasvolsky, *Economic Nationalism of the Danubian States* (New York: The Macmillan Company, 1928). A thorough study of the nationality question and the failure of the minority treaties between the wars is C. A. Macartney, *National States and National Minorities* (New York: Russell & Russell Publishers, 1968; first published in 1934). Right-wing and fascist movements which flourished in East Central Europe are surveyed in Hans Rogger and Eugen Weber (eds.), **The European Right, A Historical Profile* (Berkeley and Los Angeles: University of California Press, 1966) and Peter F. Sugar (ed.), *Native Fascism in the Successor States*, 1918–1945 (Santa Barbara, Calif.: ABC-CLIO,. Inc., 1971).

The literature on the First Austrian Republic is plentiful in both English and German, but usually reflects the deep ideological divisions of the period. A satisfactory account of the whole period has yet to be written in English, but in German, Heinrich Benedikt (ed.), *Geschichte der Republik Österreich* (Vienna: Verlag für Geschichte und Politik, 1954), is both objective and comprehensive. Walter Goldinger's contribution on political history has been reprinted in 1962 under the same title and by the same publisher. An early work which still contains useful insights, especially on political factionalism, is Franz Borkenau, *Austria and After* (London: Faber & Faber, 1938). By far the most detailed study of the period is Charles A. Gulick, *Austria from Habsburg to Hitler,* 2 vols. (Berkeley and Los Angeles: University of California Press, 1948). Gulick is passionately pro-Socialist and sees the Social Democrats as the only "true democrats" in the Republic. Mary Mac-Donald, *The Republic of Austria, 1918–1934, A Study in the Failure of a Democratic Government* (London: Oxford University Press, 1946) is a perceptive analysis. The critical early years of the Republic are covered by David F. Strong, in *Austria, October 1918–March 1919* (New York: Columbia University Press, 1939), which is exceedingly dry, but helpful on economic conditions. Klemens von Klemperer in his article "Austria, 1918–1920, Revolution by Consensus," *Orbis,* X (Winter, 1967), pp. 1061–1081, stresses the moderate nature of the Austrian revolution and the tragic consequences of the breakup of the coalition government.

No adequate study exists in any Western language on the First Czechoslovak Republic. Frederick D. Heyman, **Poland and Czechoslovakia* (Englewood Cliffs, N.J.: Prentice-Hall, Inc., 1966) contains an elementary chapter on the interwar years. A detailed and scholarly work on a rather specialized topic is Piotr S. Wandyczk, *France and Her Eastern Allies, 1919–1925, French-Czechoslovak-Polish Relations from the Paris Peace Conference to Locarno* (Minneapolis: University of Minnesota Press, 1962). A sentimental and very pro-Czech general overview of Czechoslovak history and culture is Robert J. Kerner (ed.), *Czechoslovakia* (Berkeley and Los Angeles: University of California Press, 1945). A much more critical study of a more limited subject is Edward Taborsky, *Czechoslovak Democracy at Work* (London: George Allen & Unwin, Ltd., 1945), which points out the weaknesses of proportional representation in Czechoslovakia and the lack of a constructive opposition.

C. A. Macartney's prolific pen is one of the few to describe the history of interwar Hungary in a Western language. *October Fifteenth, A History of Modern Hungary, 1929–1945*, 2 vols. (Edinburgh: At the University Press, 2d ed., 1961) is a political narrative. The fate of Magyar minorities abroad is reviewed by the same author in *Hungary and Her Successors, 1919–1937* (New York: Oxford University Press, 1968; first published in 1937). Another scholarly work dealing with interwar minority questions is Dennison I. Rusinow, *Italy's Austrian Heritage, 1919–1946* (New York: Oxford University Press, 1969), which argues that Italy's annexations were just as detrimental for that country's domestic and foreign affairs as they were for the new minorities.

On Poland between the wars the best book is easily Hans Roos, *A History of Modern Poland* (New York: Alfred A. Knopf, Inc., 1966). Bernadotte E. Schmitt (ed.), *Poland* (Berkeley and Los Angeles: University of California Press, 1945) is uncritically pro-Polish and dated. A good brief factual survey of Yugoslavia is Stephen Clissold (ed.), *A Short History of Yugoslavia* (London: Cambridge University Press, 1966). A more general, but less scholarly study is Robert J. Kerner (ed.), *Yugoslavia* (Berkeley and Los Angeles: University of California Press, 1944).

The causes of the Second World War have not produced a controversy of anything like the same magnitude as World War I. The standard interpretation arising from the Nürnberg Trials and before was that a world war was deliberately instigated by Hitler and his henchmen. This view was challenged in 1961 by A. J. P. Taylor in **The Origins of the Second World War* (New York: Fawcett World Library, Premier Books, 2d ed., 1966). Taylor sees Hitler as a traditional European statesman whose rational goal was to restore Germany to its position at the time of the Treaty of Brest Litovsk. More recent works such as Keith Eubank, **The Origins of World War II* (New York: Thomas Y. Crowell Company, 1969) deny the traditional nature of Hitler's diplomacy while admitting that Hitler did not want a *world* war in 1939 but miscalculated on the West's determination to fight for Poland.

The same author maintains in *Munich* (Norman, Okla.: University of Oklahoma Press, 1963) that the West was neither militarily nor psychologically prepared for war in 1938. A second brief survey of the causes of the war is Christopher Thorne, *The Approach of War, 1938–1939* (New York: St. Martin's Press, Inc., 1968).

Of the more specialized works dealing with problems related to Nazi imperialism, Antonin Basch, *The Danube Basin and the German Economic Sphere* (New York: Columbia University Press, 1943) unveils Germany's economic penetration of East Central Europe and the West's corresponding complacency. The most recent and reliable book on the *Anschluss* movement is Jürgen Gehl, *Austria, Germany and the Anschluss, 1931–1938* (London: Oxford University Press, 1963), which emphasizes the last-minute improvised nature of the *Anschluss*. In addition to Eubank's study of the Munich Conference, a broader work on Czech-Sudeten developments is Radomir Luza, *The Transfer of the Sudeten Germans: A Study of Czech-German Relations, 1933–1962* (New York: New York University Press, 1964), which is distinctly pro-Czech, but scholarly. A detailed account also from the Czech point of view is Boris Celovsky, *Das Münchner Abkommen von 1938* (Stuttgart: Deutsche Verlags-Anstalt, 1958). The diplomacy of Colonel Józef Beck has been reexamined and defended by Anna Cienciala in *Poland and the Western Powers, 1938–1939, A Study of the Interdependence of Eastern and Western Europe* (London: Routledge & Kegan Paul; Toronto: University of Toronto Press, 1968).

Index